Creative
ART OF
EMBROIDERY

THE EMBROIDERERS' GUILD NSW INC.

A J.B. Fairfax Press Publication

CONTENTS

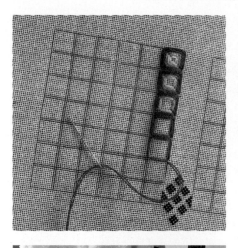

EDITORIAL
Managing Editor: Judy Poulos
Editorial Assistant: Ella Martin
Editorial Coordinator: Margaret Kelly
Photography: Andrew Elton
Styling: Kathy Tripp
Illustrations: Lesley Griffith

DESIGN AND PRODUCTION
Manager: Anna Maguire
Design: Jenny Nossal
Cover Design: Jenny Pace
Layout: Lulu Dougherty, Sheridan Packer
Picture Editor: Stacey Strickland

Published by J.B. Fairfax Press Pty Limited
80-82 McLachlan Ave, Rushcutters Bay 2011
Australia
A.C.N. 003 738 430

Formatted by J.B. Fairfax Press Pty Limited

Printed by Toppan Printing Company,
Singapore
© J.B. Fairfax Press Pty Limited 1996
This book is copyright. No part may be
reproduced by any process without the
written permission of the publisher. Enquiries
should be made in writing to the publisher.

JBFP 443

CREATIVE ART OF EMBROIDERY
ISBN 1 86343 276 0

CONTENTS

INTRODUCTION

Embroidery is many things to many people – pastime, creative outlet, practical decoration or exercise of skill. Whether they be young or old, male or female, it is true to say that most embroiderers are enticed by the sheer joy of decorating fabric with needle and thread.

For many centuries, embroidery was the province of a privileged few. It was found mostly on church vestments, royal robes and the dress of the aristocracy, and was usually executed by professional embroiderers. With the increased availability of fabric and threads to middle-class families, embroidery began to appear on household linens and 'special occasion' clothing. These days, embroidery has evolved from these beginnings to an art form practised across the entire community.

The Embroiderers' Guild NSW Inc. was formed in 1957 with a membership of seven women. Today, the Guild's membership is well over two thousand men, women and children.

With its aims focused on increasing knowledge and skill, the Embroiderers' Guild and its members are happy to share their love of embroidery through the pages of *Art of Embroidery*.

So, take up your needle and thread, and happy embroidering!

Coralie Lewin
President
The Embroiderers' Guild NSW Inc.

THE CONTRIBUTORS

ROSIE ANSLEY

Experienced in many techniques of embroidery, Rosie continues to explore new areas as well as revisiting old favourites, such as her blackwork decorations on page 64.

MARGARET BROWNE

In her work, Margaret is particularly inspired by the countryside surrounding her home in the Southern Highlands of New South Wales and the native flora. Her delicate organza bag on page 42 is embellished with a beautiful white waratah.

VALERIE CRAVEN

Valerie has a great love of painting as well as embroidery; no doubt the reason for her very painterly approach to her project on page 39.

MARGARET CRAWFORD

Margaret enjoys both hand- and machine-embroidery, specialising in the latter. Her interest in machine-embroidered clothing is evidenced by her dramatic vest on page 17.

BARBARA CURRAN

Tassels have always been popular with craftspeople and especially with embroiderers. Barbara used her skill with macramé to embellish the tassel on page 70.

RONA GIBSON

Experienced in many fine embroidery techniques, Rona particularly loves shadow embroidery. She often gathers inspiration for her work from the flowers in her country garden and this is clearly evident on page 20.

JEAN HERRING

Jean has many years of experience as an embroiderer and a teacher of a wide range of embroidery techniques. Her embroidered landscape on page 57 employs a variety of techniques on a base of layered fabric.

ANNETTE HINDE

Annette is one of the Guild's talented tutors. At present, she is concentrating on stumpwork, giving it a fresh Australian flavour, such as the bottlebrush on page 12.

HEATHER JOYNES

Heather is one of the Guild's tutors and the author of several books. She is particularly knowledgeable about the history of embroidery and its conservation, the subject of her text on page 63.

LAURA LEVERTON

Laura is a very experienced traditional embroiderer. She particularly favours counted-thread embroidery and her skill is apparent in her contribution to this book on page 29.

JANET LUCE

An experienced embroiderer, Janet exercises her particular skill with fine counted-thread techniques to embellish garments, such as the linen blouse on page 67.

EFFIE MITROFANIS

A tutor of hand-embroidery, author of three books and talented embroiderer, Effie is constantly experimenting with new directions. For her three projects in this book, (the canvas purse on page 8, the snow crystals cushion on page 50, and the pansy tablecloth on page 26) she has drawn inspiration from the Embroiderers' Guild collection.

ONITA POLLITT

The mother of a young family, Onita has managed to maintain her interest in fine hand-embroidery, heirloom sewing and smocking, while juggling her family responsibilities. Onita trimmed the charming basket on page 54 with panels of counterchange smocking. In her candlewicking cushion on page 60, Onita has given a familiar technique a new twist with colour.

JANICE RAWLINSON

A tutor with the Embroiderers' Guild, Janice specialises in gold thread embroidery and has a particular expertise in creating original designs for metallic thread work. Her dramatic paperweight on page 36 is a testimony to her skill.

HELEN WHELAN

A tutor for the Guild in canvas embroidery, Helen has a talent for using a variety of textures and dyed threads to create wonderful effects that are not difficult for a less experienced embroiderer to emulate, as seen in her little picture on page 45.

THE EMBROIDERERS' GUILD COLLECTION

The Embroiderers' Guild NSW has a collection of embroideries encompassing a wide variety of techniques and items. Most of the articles have been donated by members or friends of the Guild, while others have been purchased from galleries and exhibitions. In 1957, the founding members of the Embroiderers' Guild realised that a collection such as this would be an important resource. The Collection Committee very early established a high standard for the acquisition, care and storage of the collection, so that there has been a minimum of deterioration.

This year has been designated Collection Year and has seen the installation of purpose-built storage, providing very nearly museum conditions. The custodian of the collection, Marie Cavanagh, devotes a great deal of time and study to the collection. In addition, Marie travels widely to address various groups and organisations about the collection, always carrying examples with her.

Access to the collection is available by appointment to members, who find the pieces invaluable for studying stitchery and technique, as well as for inspiration.

Many of the items have a historical context, reflecting the tastes of their era or country of origin. Where possible, the committee attempts to provide provenance for pieces in the collection, often necessitating considerable research.

CANVAS PURSE

By Effie Mitrofanis

This beautiful little treasure was inspired by a Victorian piece in the Embroiderers' Guild collection. Geometric stitches are enhanced with glass beads.

MATERIALS

Note: The materials and threads used in the original purse are no longer available, so those listed are the closest available today.

30 cm (12 in) square of white Congress canvas
One skein of stranded cotton, Black
Tapestry needle, size 24
Beading needle
Beeswax
Two heaped teaspoons each of glass dress beads, medium hole: sugar-coloured, gunmetal-coloured
One skein each of DMC Medici Wool:
    Very Dark Red 8100, Dark Red 8106,
    Dark Pink 8223, Medium Pink 8224,
    Light Pink 8225
One reel of ordinary sewing cotton, size 50, White
Two metal tassel heads (available at stores selling jewellery findings)
Two skeins of DMC Stranded Cotton, Deep Burgundy 902
Four 15 mm (⅝ in) diameter metal rings
14 cm x 18 cm (5½ in x 7 in) of silk fabric for the lining
Sharp HB pencil
Rectangular roller frame

PREPARATION

See the embroidery graph on the Pull Out Pattern Sheet.

The front and back of the purse both have six rows of seven boxes each. Each box is eleven threads square and each box is separated from the next one by one thread of fabric. There is a space of seventeen threads between the boxes on the front and back of the purse. This space is stitched with cross stitch in the shape of diamonds. The cross stitch is also worked in the spaces on both sides of the boxes.

STEP ONE

Overlock or zigzag around the edges of the canvas to prevent fraying. Lace the canvas to the frame.

STEP TWO

Referring to the graph and the photograph of the prepared canvas, rule up the grid for the canvas stitches, using the sharp HB pencil and carefully counting each thread.

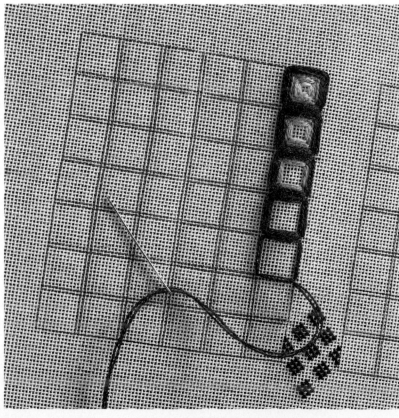

Stitching the boxes

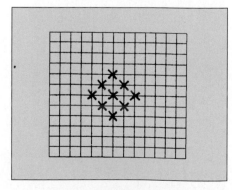

Fig. 1

EMBROIDERY

CROSS STITCH DIAMONDS

Following the graph and starting at **A**, work the cross stitch, using two strands of Black cotton in the tapestry needle (Fig. 1).

Note: The horizontal rows of diamonds are separated by five threads of canvas while the vertical rows are separated by three threads of canvas. However, on the left side of the graph, one of the rows of diamonds is separated by six threads of canvas instead of five. This extra thread allows the vertical rows of diamonds on either side of the bag to be centred.

COLOURED BOXES

The boxes are stitched in graduating colours from very dark on the outside to very light in the centre.

STEP ONE

Using two strands of Very Dark Red wool in the tapestry needle, stitch the outer edge of each box. Starting with a knot on the top of the work at **X** (Fig. 2), bring the needle out at **A**. This knot is called a waste knot and will be cut off as you work close to it.

STEP TWO

Following figure 2 and working from right to left, stitch four back stitches: **A-B-C**, **C-A-D**, **D-B-C**, **C-D-E**. **E** begins the next box and now becomes **A**. Notice that a cross is formed at the back of each box. There are eleven threads square in the centre of the box.

For left-handers
Following figure 3 and working from left to right, stitch four back stitches: **A-B-C**, **C-A-D**, **D-B-C**, **C-D-E**. **E** begins the next box and now becomes **A**.

STEP THREE

Using two strands of Dark Red wool, stitch another four back stitches as in step two, but this time leaving a square of ten threads in the centre of the box.

STEP FOUR

Continue to work four back stitches for each colour until all five colours have been used in the following order: Very Dark Red, Dark Red, Dark Pink, Medium Pink, Light Pink. Each finished box has a small square of unstitched canvas in the centre (Fig. 4).

APPLYING THE BEADS

STEP ONE

Thread a single strand of sewing cotton in the beading needle and pull the thread through the beeswax to strengthen it. Secure the thread at the back of the work, bringing the needle and thread out at one corner of the box.

STEP TWO

Pick up six or more of the sugar-coloured beads on the thread and stitch the string of beads from that corner to the centre of the box (Fig. 5). Sew through the beads again to ensure they are secure and stable. Repeat this procedure for each corner of each box.

STEP THREE

Apply two strings containing three gunmetal-coloured beads each to the centre of the box, over the sugar-coloured beads (Fig. 6).

The beaded and embroidered canvas

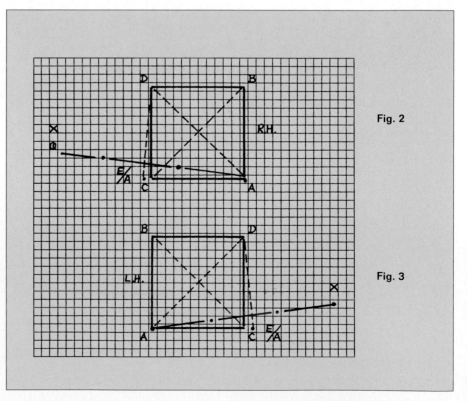

Fig. 2

Fig. 3

TASSELS

Six strings of gunmetal-coloured beads are required for each tassel. The beads on each string run for 12 cm (4¹/₂ in). The extra thread is needed to facilitate handling and finishing. Run the thread through the beeswax before adding the beads.

STEP ONE

Thread a 1 m (1¹/₈ yd) length of sewing cotton into the beading needle, double it and knot the ends together to prevent the beads falling off.

STEP TWO

Thread the gunmetal-coloured beads onto the needle for a length of 12 cm (4¹/₂ in) of beads. Remove the needle by cutting the thread near the needle and make several knots at this end to prevent the beads falling off. Repeat steps one and two until you have twelve strings of beads.

STEP THREE

Pin or tape one end of one string of beads to a surface, such as a table. Ensure that the beads are situated in the middle of the thread, then twist the cotton until it is tightly twisted. Double the thread over so that the two knotted ends meet, allowing the beads to twist. Knot the two ends together. Repeat this step for the other eleven strings.

STEP FOUR

To form one bunch, tie six twisted bead strings together by wrapping and stitching the ends together with sewing cotton. Thread the needle up through the tulip-shaped cap, then stitch the cap to the front of the purse, allowing 4 mm (³/₁₆ in) of thread between the top of the cap and the purse so that the tassel hangs freely. Sew backwards and forwards between the tassel and the purse several times to secure.

MAKING UP

STEP ONE

Remove the canvas from the frame. Cut out the purse leaving approximately 1.5 cm (⁵/₈ in) seam allowance all around. Fold over the seam allowances on all four sides of the purse and hemstitch it in place.

STEP TWO

Stitch the four metal rings to the top of the purse, leaving a gap of approximately 5 cm (2 in) between the two rings and placing each ring approximately 2 cm (³/₄ in) from the sides of the purse.

LINING

Cut out the lining slightly bigger than the finished size of the purse. Fold in a seam allowance all around so that the lining is slightly smaller than the purse, then pin the lining in place on the back of the purse and hemstitch it to all four sides. Fold the purse in half and slipstitch the two sides together.

TWISTED CORD AND HANDLE

STEP ONE

Cut four 2 m (2¹/₄ yd) lengths of Black stranded cotton to make a twisted cord that is approximately 70 cm (28 in) finished length. (See page 70 for how to make a twisted cord.) Make two. Starting on one side of the purse, 1.5 cm (⁵/₈ in) from the top, slipstitch the cord to the purse, taking it around the top and down the other side for 1.5 cm (⁵/₈ in). Take it back up to the top and around the other side to meet the beginning. Finish off the end of the cord by stitching and trimming the end, then tucking it under the beginning of the cord to conceal it.

STEP TWO

Thread the other cord through the four rings at the top of the purse to form the handle. Knot the two ends together and trim the loose ends to approximately 2 cm (³/₄ in) for a small tassel.

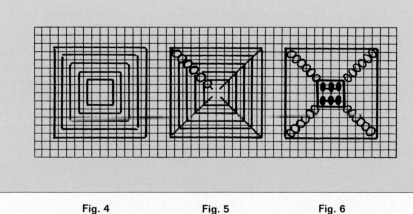

Fig. 4   Fig. 5   Fig. 6

The Victorian purse

BOTTLEBRUSH PAPERWEIGHT

By Annette Hinde

Traditional stumpwork has been given a fresh Australian flavour
with this design of native bottlebrushes.

MATERIALS

10 cm (4 in) embroidery hoop

20 cm (8 in) square of washed calico
or homespun

20 cm (8 in) square of Pellon or a
similar thin wadding

20 cm (8 in) square of silk or polyester
satin fabric in the colour of your
choice for the background

10 cm (4 in) of 12 mm ($^1/_2$ in) wide
double-sided satin ribbon in a green
that is similar in colour to DMC 937

DMC Stranded Cotton: Dark Taupe
840, Green 937, Light Brown 435,
Bright Red 666, Dark Crimson 321,
Butter Yellow 744

DMC Flower Thread, Green 937

Tapestry needles, sizes 26 and 22

Chenille needle, size 22

Crewel needles, sizes 8 and 5

Straw or milliners needle, size 8

2B pencil

Strong cardboard

Thick thread

PVA white craft glue

Glass paperweight and base

Tweezers

PREPARATION

See the embroidery design on page 16.

STEP ONE

Accurately copy the outline of the
design onto the calico with the pencil.
The drawing will appear as the reverse
of the completed embroidery.

STEP TWO

Place the background fabric, Pellon
and calico in the embroidery hoop so
the traced design shows on the back.
The fabric must be held taut in the
hoop at all times. Once you have
started, do not take your work out of
the hoop.

STEP THREE

Working from the underside of the
hoop with the calico and the traced
lines facing you, work a running stitch
down the lines of the stem, using one
strand of the Dark Taupe. Work around
the outline of the leaves and their
stems in running stitch, using one
strand of Green. Baste around the
outline circle. This stitching will give
the design outlines on the front of
your work.

EMBROIDERY

Note: Anchor all the threads in the
calico fabric. Do not use knots which
may be visible in the finished piece.

STEP ONE

Using four strands of Dark Taupe and
starting at the tip of each stem, work
in chain stitch down the two stems.
Using a tapestry needle, whip these
chain stitches with four threads: one
Dark Taupe, one Light Brown and two
Green. Note that the whipping stitches
do not go through the fabric, but pass
between the fabric and the chain
stitches.

STEP TWO

Using one strand of Green, starting
at the base of the leaf and working
towards the tip, fill the leaf with rows
of stem stitch. Work the leaf stem
in Green stem stitch.

STEP THREE

For the open brush, work the side tips
in three long chain stitches, worked on
top of each other, using one strand of
Green. The central tip is three long
chain stitches in Green, worked on top
of each other. For the partly open
brush, work the side tips in three long
chain stitches in Green, worked on top
of each other. The central tip is a picot
stitch worked with two strands of Light
Brown (see the Stitch Guide on page 15).

STEP FOUR

The position of the buds is indicated by
the triangles on the drawn design on
the calico. Work the buds in raised cup
stitch, starting at the tip of the stem and
using the flower thread or two strands
of Green stranded cotton (see the
Stitch Guide).

STEP FIVE

Work the partially open bud as for the
bud, completing one row of detached
buttonhole stitch. Thread the chenille
needle with three strands of Bright Red,
three strands of Dark Crimson and
one strand of Butter Yellow. Bring the
needle out in the centre of the bud and
take the thread down to the back,
leaving a loop 1-2 mm ($^1/_{32}$-$^1/_{16}$ in) high.
Work the rest of the bud in detached
buttonhole stitch around the loop of
Bright Red thread.

Pewter Inkwell and Pen from Mosman Antique Centre, Mosman NSW

STEP SIX

For the flat stamens or tufts, thread the chenille needle with four strands of Bright Red, four strands of Dark Crimson and one strand of Butter Yellow. Bring the thread to the front of the work 2 mm (¹/₁₆ in) from the stem at the positions indicated by the dots on the calico drawing. Bring to the front a second needle, threaded with the flower thread or two strands of Green and wrap it tightly around the Bright Red, Dark Crimson and Butter Yellow threads four times. Take the Green thread to the back. Take the Bright Red, Dark Crimson and Butter Yellow threads to the back, 6 mm (¹/₄ in) from where they emerged, two at a time and fanning out from the centre. Regroup the threads and repeat this step along the stem.

STEP SEVEN

For the leaning stamens, thread the needle with four strands of Bright Red, four strands of Dark Crimson and one strand of Butter Yellow. Bring the threads up between the flat stamens and the stem, but not in line with the flat stamens. Take the threads to the back, leaving a loop of threads 1 cm (³/₈ in) long. Bring up a second needle threaded with the flower thread and wrap it around the Bright Red, Dark Crimson and Butter Yellow threads four times. Take the Green thread to the back so that the stamen is leaning out from the stem.

STEP EIGHT

For the upright tufts, bring the Bright Red thread up on one side of the stem and take it down on the other side of the stem leaving a loop of threads 1 cm (³/₈ in) long. Wrap the Bright Red threads with the Green thread as before, then take the Green thread to the back through the stem. When the work is completed, slide a needle through the loops and trim them to 6 mm (¹/₄ in) long.

STEP NINE

For the raised leaves, mark out the leaf shape on the double-sided satin ribbon. Using one strand of Green and starting at the leaf tip, work a row of back stitch down the central vein, leaving a tail of thread at the leaf base. Paint both sides of the ribbon with a solution of sixty per cent PVA white craft glue and forty per cent water, covering the leaf shape and the area around it. When the ribbon is dry, cut out the shape and attach it to the work with the tail of thread. If the leaf is not stiff enough, paint it again with the glue solution, before you attach it. Manipulate the leaves into position with tweezers.

MAKING UP

STEP ONE

Cut a circle from the cardboard, just smaller than the base of the paper-weight.

STEP TWO

While the work is still in the hoop, use the strong thread to sew a gathering stitch 1 cm (³/₈ in) from the outside basting line. Remove the work from the hoop and cut around just outside the gathering line. Place the embroidery over the cardboard circle, then pull up the gathering thread and tie off the ends. Secure the embroidery in the paperweight base with a spot of glue.

The flat embroidery follows the stitched outline

14

STITCH GUIDE

RAISED CUP STITCH

Work a triangle of straight stitch to form the framework (Fig. 1).

Work detached buttonhole stitch over the straight stitch, pulling the thread upwards (Fig. 2).

For the next and following rows, continue to work detached buttonhole stitch into the loops of the preceding row, gradually decreasing the number of stitches so the cup closes (Fig. 3).

NEEDLE-WOVEN PICOT

Insert a fine needle into the fabric, the length of the picot tip away from the base. Bring the needle out at **A**, take it down at **B**, passing it under the tip of the needle, but not through the fabric. Bring the thread out at **C** (Fig. 4).

Wrap the thread around the needle and give it a firm pull (Fig. 5).

Slide the needle under the centre thread and give it a firm pull (Fig. 6).

Slide the needle over the outer loop and under the centre in one direction (Fig. 6), then reverse the direction and go under the outer loop and over the centre, and so on. As you weave in this way, push the threads firmly up to the point of the picot.

Fig. 1

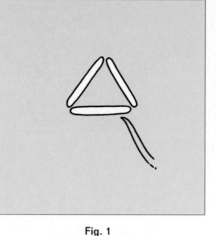

Fig. 2

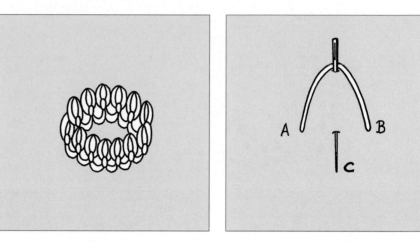

Fig. 3

Fig. 4

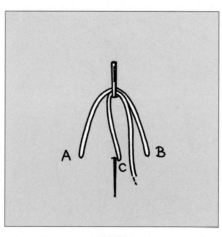

Fig. 5

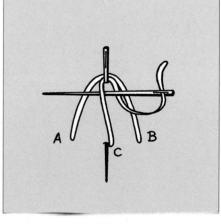

Fig. 6

15

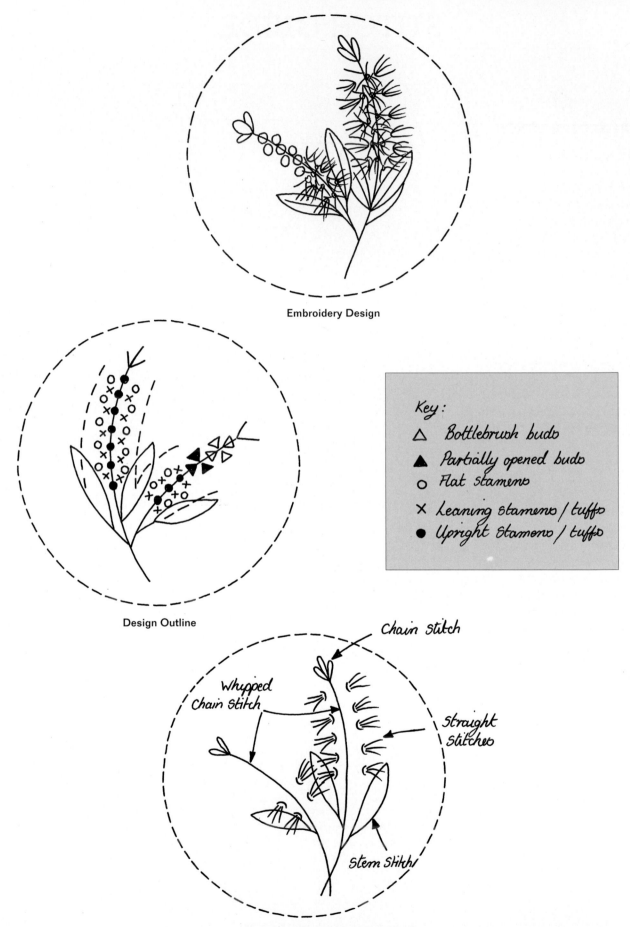

Embroidery Design

Design Outline

Key:
△ Bottlebrush buds
▲ Partially opened buds
○ Flat stamens
✕ Leaning stamens / tufts
● Upright stamens / tufts

Chain stitch

Whipped Chain stitch

Straight stitches

Stem Stitch

Flat embroidery on the background

16

MACHINE-EMBROIDERED VEST

By Margaret Crawford

The inspiration for this vest comes from the vibrant colours
of Australian landscapes – in this instance the harmony that a
radiant sunset brings to the earth and plains as we move into night.

Note: The project is suitable for beginners as it uses one simple free machine-sewing technique and straight sewing to apply the braid and embellishments.

MATERIALS

Commercial vest pattern (any pattern without shaping is suitable)

50 cm (20 in) of fabric for the back

20 cm (8 in) each of five fabrics for the front (choose some plains, as well as some patterns, including polyester, silk, organza, velvet etc)

60 cm (24 in) of polycotton in a colour coordinating with the five fabrics for the base fabric

60 cm (24 in) of paper-backed fusible webbing

Beka Metafil needle, size 80

10 m (11 yd) of metallic coloured braid

One reel of Madeira Carat Thread, no. 228

One reel of Madeira Metallic Thread, no. 24

One reel of Madeira Rayon Thread, no. 1126

One reel of Mettler Metrosene Thread, no. 663

One skein of DMC Stranded Cotton, Gold 780

Crewel embroidery needle

Six large and ten small star buttons with shanks

Small piece of cardboard, 7 cm (2³/₄ in) square

Lining fabric to complete the vest as per the pattern

Pressing cloth, appliqué mat or baking paper

Note: Protect your eyes when doing free machine-embroidery. If you do not normally wear glasses whilst working, wear a pair of the protective glasses available from opticians.

BEFORE YOU BEGIN

The concept of this project is to make up a fabric before constructing a vest, using a commercial vest pattern. Instructions are for making up the fabric only. The quantities of fabric and threads given are for a small size. If you wish to make a larger size, make the appropriate adjustments to the quantities.

PREPARATION

STEP ONE

Cut a piece of the back fabric, 60 cm x 70 cm (24 in x 27¹/₂ in). This is equivalent to the size of two vest fronts plus an allowance for shrinkage during sewing. Do not cut out the vest fronts at this stage.

STEP TWO

Cut 60 cm x 70 cm (24 in x 27¹/₂ in) from the paper-backed fusible webbing. Using the iron on a moderate non-steam setting, attach the webbing to the wrong side of the back fabric. Remove the paper backing.

STEP THREE

Using scissors or a rotary cutter, cut the coordinating fabrics into 70 cm (27¹/₂ in) long strips. (Our vest has strips cut in the following widths: gold metallic, two strips each 5 cm (2 in) wide; brown patterned, two strips each 9 cm (3¹/₂ in) wide; tan plain, two strips each 5.5 cm (2¹/₄ in) wide; brown multi, two strips each 6 cm (2³/₈ in) wide; light tan plain, one strip 9 cm (3¹/₂ in) wide.)

FABRIC DESIGN

STEP ONE

Place the base fabric with the fusible web face upwards on the ironing board. Place the fabric strips on top, face upwards and butted against each other in the following order: gold, brown, tan, brown multi, light tan, brown multi, light tan, brown, gold. Cover them with a pressing cloth, appliqué mat or baking paper and press.

STEP TWO

Wind the bobbin with the rayon thread and insert the Beka needle for metallic sewing. Thread the sewing machine with the metallic thread. Set up the sewing machine as follows: top tension – normal to partially loose; bobbin tension – normal; stitch length – zero; stitch width – zigzag, anywhere from 1 to maximum. Install the darning foot and lower the feed dogs (or cover them with the cover plate).

STEP THREE

Place the fabric under the foot of the machine, on the point where two fabric strips meet. Sew on the spot, where the thread comes up from the bobbin. Cut off the ends of the bobbin and top threads.

STEP FOUR

Holding the fabric tightly in both hands, move your hands in a zigzag motion down the strips. Because you have the feed dogs lowered, the length of the stitches are under your control. You determine the length by how slowly or quickly you move your fabric. Do not worry if your threads break, simply rethread and start again from that spot. Continue in this way until all the edges have been stitched, then press.

STEP FIVE

Change to normal machine-sewing mode. Set the machine to a straight running stitch with a length 2.5, and sew down the centre of the metallic braid on the tan-coloured strips. Do this twice on each tan strip.

STEP SIX

Lay out the front pattern piece on the fabric you have created and cut out the vest fronts.

SCROLLS

Using 50 cm (20 in) lengths of metallic braid, the crewel embroidery needle and the rayon thread, make four braid scrolls as shown in figure 1. Wind one end first, slipstitching as you go, tie off, then wind the other end in the same way. Slipstitch the completed scrolls to the vest fronts.

TASSELS

STEP ONE

Wrap the threads around the cardboard square in the following sequence: stranded cotton, seventeen wraps; braid, seven wraps; stranded cotton, thirteen wraps; metallic sewing thread, twenty wraps. When the wrapping is completed, tie it off at the top, using a double knot or reef knot of braid, placing one end of the knot back into the skirt of the tassel. Cut through the wraps at the bottom and remove the tassel from the cardboard. Using the braid, tie a double knot or reef knot, 15 mm ($^5/_8$ in) from the top of the tassel to form the head. Trim the tassel bottoms.

STEP TWO

Pass the top cord of the tassel through the shank of two star buttons. Tie a third button to the top of the top thread, then sew the tassel and buttons to the vest.

TO COMPLETE

STEP ONE

Sew the rest of the star buttons randomly over the front of the vest.

STEP TWO

Assemble the vest and the lining as per the pattern instructions.

HINTS

• Clean and oil your sewing machine before starting work.

• To save time, thread up several bobbins before you commence sewing.

• Select fabrics that have interesting texture and look at the back of the fabric – it might be more interesting than the front.

• Instead of buttons, use jewellery, charms or other found objects to decorate the vest.

• Change your sewing machine needles regularly – eight hours sewing time is a good measure to use for assessing when to change.

• With leftover fabric, you can make a belt to match, a small purse, or cards.

Joined fabric ready for embroidery

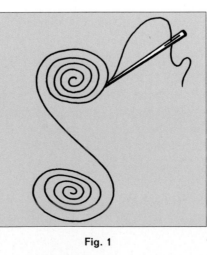

Fig. 1

Embroidery and appliquéd scroll

Dummy from Henmarks, Surry Hills NSW

19

SHADOW-EMBROIDERED SHOWER CAP

By Rona Gibson

The charm of shadow embroidery is apparent in this very feminine shower cap. Elements of the embroidery design have been taken to decorate the hanky sachet and the lavender bag.

MATERIALS

60 cm (24 in) of fabric, such as organdie, organza, batiste, voile, fine silk or terylene

50 cm (20 in) of showerproof fabric

1.9 m (2¹/₈ yd) of 1.5-2 cm (⁵/₈–³/₄ in) wide lace edging

Fine machine-sewing thread, such as no. 30 or no. 50 machine-embroidery thread in a colour to match the lace and the fabric

50 cm (20 in) of 5 mm (¹/₄ in) wide elastic

Embroidery hoop

DMC Stranded Cotton: Pinks 760, 761, 776, 819, 963, 3354, 3688; Greens 523, 524, 772, 928; Blue 3752; Yellow 744

Crewel needle, size 9 (a sharp, straw or between needle is also suitable if it is more comfortable to use)

Water-soluble marker pen or pencil

BEFORE YOU BEGIN

The basic stitch is a closed herringbone stitch, worked from the wrong side of the fabric with no spaces between the stitches. The areas of the design to be shaded are stitched from side to side, producing a continuous outline to the shapes on the right side of the work.

A small back stitch, worked alternately on each side of the design on the right side of the fabric can also be used. This is called a double back stitch. It is essential that each succeeding stitch is taken back into the same hole as the previous stitch. It is easier to achieve this continuity of outline working from the right side.

Any veins, stamens or shading lines within an outline are usually best stitched before the shadow stitch, and can be worked without a frame or hoop.

Note: Read all the instructions before you begin.

PREPARATION

See the embroidery designs on the Pull Out Pattern Sheet .

STEP ONE

Outline the shape of a 50 cm (20 in) diameter circle on the fabric with a row of straight or zigzag machine stitches to stabilise the fabric. Cut away the surplus fabric and mark the centre of the circle by finger-pressing it into quarters.

STEP TWO

Trace the design onto the fabric, using the marker pen or pencil. Place the circle of fabric in the embroidery hoop, stretching the fabric taut and keeping the grains straight.

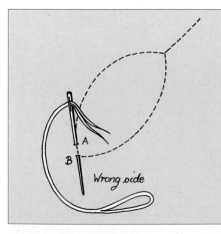

Fig. 1

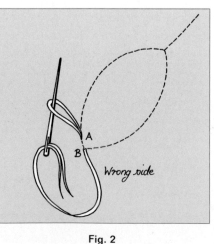

Fig. 2

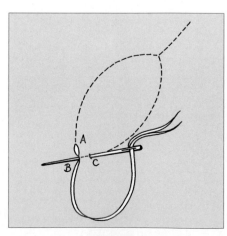

Fig. 3

Chair from Cane & Cottage Antiques, Lindfield NSW

EMBROIDERY

The embroidery is worked in the sequence and colours indicated on the embroidery design. Two strands are used for all the shadow embroidery, using stitches that are 1.5-2 mm (approximately $^1/_{16}$ in) long. Shade lines and leaf veins are worked with one strand of thread. The specific instructions given below are for working a leaf. Simply use the same method in the appropriate colours for working the other elements of the design.

STEP ONE

Cut a thread approximately 80 cm (32 in) long. Double this thread and pass the two cut ends through the eye of the needle. Working on the wrong side of the fabric and using closed herring-bone stitch, take a stitch to the point on one side of the first leaf outline **A** to **B** (Fig. 1). Next, pass the needle through the loop end of the thread (Fig. 2) and draw up the stitch – firmly, but not tight enough to pull the fabric and create obvious holes.

STEP TWO

Still working from the wrong side, on the opposite side of the leaf, take a stitch of the same length from **C** to **B** (Fig. 3). Return to the first side and stitch from **D** to **A** (Fig. 4). Continue in this manner until the leaf shape is completely filled with stitches of the same length and tightness (Figs 5-7).

Hint: Keep dropping the needle containing the working threads so that they will untwist. A better coverage of shadow is obtained when the threads lie beside, rather than twisted around, each other. Hold the worked area up to the light frequently to check that there are no unwanted shadows or open space in the shaded areas.

STEP THREE

If the thread remaining is sufficient to work the stem, take the needle through to the right side at the point where the leaf joins the stem. Working now from the right side, take one running stitch, then back stitch to the end of the stem (Fig. 8). Make sure all the stitches are the same length on the right side. Finish off the thread in back stitch on the wrong side by stitching over and over the stitches about five times, leaving the last two loops loose (Fig. 9). Pass the needle back through these two loops, drop the needle, hold the needle thread and the fabric firmly between the thumb and fingers of one hand and pull the last loop worked. Lastly, pull the needle thread and cut off the excess thread.

STEP FOUR

To finish off threads behind the shadow work (closed herringbone or double back stitch), take a straight stitch directly behind the last back stitch, a little shorter than the back stitch, picking up the fabric only (Fig. 10). Next, pass the needle under one of the crossed threads, take a second straight

stitch behind the next back stitch and continue until about five stitches have been worked, then cut the thread (Fig. 11). The finishing stitches must be invisible from the right side of the work.

If you prefer to work in double back stitch, commence and finish as for closed herringbone stitch, and work a back stitch alternately on each side of the outlined design, working all stitches from the right side (Figs 12, 13, 14, 15, 16). These stitches can be worked as a stab stitch or with the needle slanting from side to side.

CIRCLES AND OVALS

For circles and oval shapes, such as the daisy centres, back stitch the line in the middle of the oval from **A** to **B**, then take a back stitch on each side of where this line meets the outline (**C** to **B** and **D** to **B**) (Fig. 17). Continue back stitching from side to side. The last two stitches meet, worked into the same hole at the opposite side of the oval.

DAISY PETALS

Commence close to the centre and work out to the tip of the petal. Stitch and weave the thread on the wrong side of the fabric, down to the centre on one side of the petal, as for the leaves. Work the petals of the half-open daisy in the same way, then work the calyx and stem.

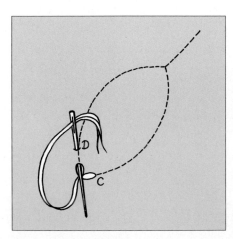

Fig. 4

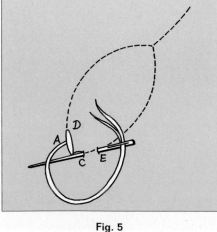

Fig. 5

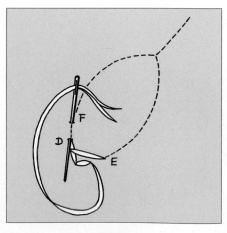

Fig. 6

OVERLAPPING AREAS

Use this method where one section of the design overlaps another, or two adjacent sections have an outline in common, for example, the side view of the single rose. Work the top on the centre petal first, then work the side petal by taking one back stitch on the outline and passing the needle under one or two threads of the adjoining petal on the other side (Fig. 18).

ROSE LEAVES

Work the veins and stems with two strands first, then work the leaves, taking one stitch only to form the indentation in the edge.

STAMENS

The stamens in the single roses have been worked in pistil stitch, using one strand. Alternatively, you could use a straight stitch, with or without a knot at the end (Figs 19, 20, 21).

MAKING UP

STEP ONE

Remove the embroidered circle of fabric from the hoop and lay it flat. Shape the lace edging to fit the outline of the circle of fabric by drawing up one of the threads in the straight edge of the lace until the shaped edge lies flat at the edge of the circle. Baste the lace into position and pin the ends of the lace together, matching the pattern in the lace.

STEP TWO

Cut one end of the lace to 6 mm (¼ in) outside the pin and the other end to 1 cm (⅜ in). Turn under the longer end and hem it down over the shorter end, using the fine thread and small stitches. Turn to the underside of the lace edging, carefully remove the pin, then fold and hem this in the same way.

STEP THREE

Using the fine machine-sewing thread, straight stitch the lace to the fabric, inside the gathered edge of the lace. To prevent the fabric stretching or puckering when stitching across the bias grains, you may find it necessary to have strips of tissue paper or unwaxed greaseproof paper under the fabric while attaching the lace. Tear away the paper before the next step.

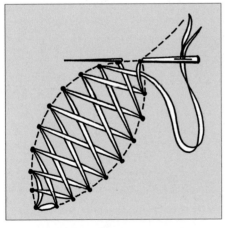

Fig. 7

Fig. 8

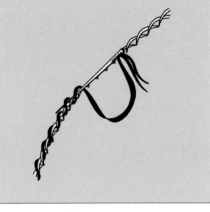

Fig. 9

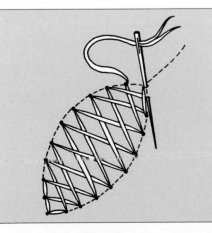

Fig. 10

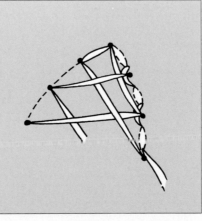

Fig. 11

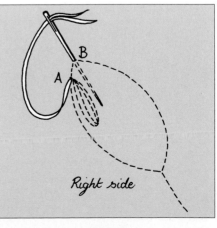

Fig. 12

STEP FOUR

Remove any pins or basting threads and finger-press the fabric edge back and away from the lace. Machine zigzag stitch from the right side over the inner lace edge and folded edge of the fabric underneath. Carefully cut away the excess fabric.

STEP FIVE

Mark the outline of the circle on the showerproof fabric with one row of straight machine-stitching. Cut away the excess fabric, approximately 1 mm (¹/₃₂ in) from the line. Overstitch the cut edge and straight stitching with a small zigzag stitch.

STEP SIX

Divide both circles (embroidered fabric and showerproof fabric) into four equal sections on the straight grains. Mark the lines with pins or

basting. Place the showerproof circle underneath the embroidered circle so that the centres match and the quarter markings of one fall to the centre of the quarter markings of the other. Thus the bias of one circle will be directly on the straight grain of the other. Secure them with pins or basting.

STEP SEVEN

Machine-stitch from the showerproof fabric side, using a straight medium-length stitch close to the finished edge. Leave an opening of approximately 6 mm (¹/₄ in) in the stitching for the elastic. Work a second row of straight machine-stitching the width of the elastic plus 3 mm (¹/₈ in) inside the first row to form the casing for the elastic. Cut an appropriate length of elastic and thread it through the casing. Overlap the ends for 2 cm (³/₄ in) and topstitch the join.

HINTS

• It is important to take small stitches behind the back stitches of an outline so that the thread end will remain at the edge rather than work its way towards the centre of the worked space where it could be conspicuous from the right side.

• When finishing off working threads or joining one section to another (such as overlapping petals) take care not to open up spaces between crossed threads forming the shadow/s.

• If you are working with an uneven number of threads, commence with a waste knot by knotting the end of the thread/s together and passing the needle through the fabric from the right to the wrong side, approximately two needle lengths from the commencement of the

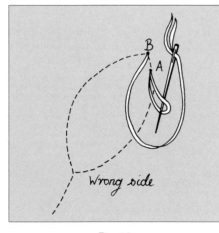

Fig. 13

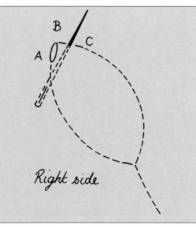

Fig. 14

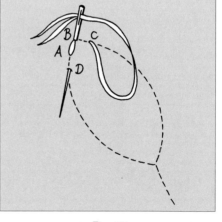

Fig. 15

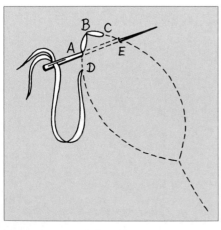

Fig. 16

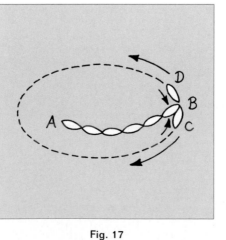

Fig. 17

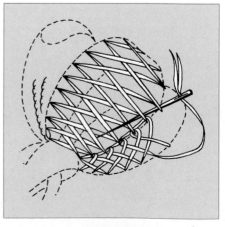

Fig. 18

stitching and away from the area to be stitched. Work shadow stitch in closed herringbone or double back stitch and, after finishing off the working thread, cut off the waste knot, thread the end/s through a needle and finish off as at the end of shadow stitching.

● To join in a new thread part-way through a shape, use either method of commencing work, depending on how many strands of thread are being used (Fig. 22).

● When the design entails working between two curved lines of similar curve but different length, the stitches are usually made smaller on the shorter/inner curve and longer on the longer/outer curve. If, however, there is a great difference between the lengths of the curves or the different-sized stitches are out of keeping with the stitching of the rest of the design, then take the same-size stitches, but double up on the inner curve every stitch or every alternate one (just as a stitch is taken behind another when finishing off a thread).

● Containers for any use, such as bags or sachets need to have a backing or lining behind the shadow embroidery so that the contents will not catch in the crossed threads of the stitching and thus distort the embroidered design.

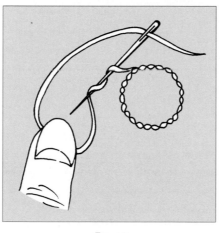

Fig. 19

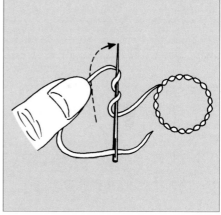

Fig. 20

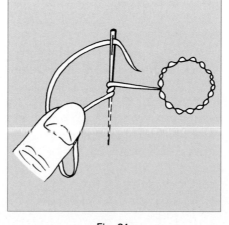

Fig. 21

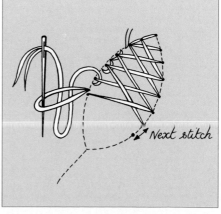

Next stitch

Fig. 22

TABLECLOTH WITH PANSIES

By Effie Mitrofanis

Pansies are old-fashioned favourites, perfectly suited to this charming tablecloth which was inspired by a cushion cover from the Embroiderers' Guild Collection.

MATERIALS

90 cm (36 in) square of ecru seeded
   calico
DMC Stranded Cotton: Greens 469,
   733, 734; Violets 3746, 333, 552;
   Yellows 742, 743
Crewel needle, size 7 or 9
5 m (5$^{1}/_{2}$ yd) of purple bias binding
5 m (5$^{1}/_{2}$ yd) of 5 cm (2 in) wide ecru
   cotton lace
Ten tea bags
2 litres (3$^{1}/_{2}$ pints) of boiling water
Half a cup of vinegar
Fabric crayons: Violet, Red, Blue, Blue/
   Green, Yellow/Green, Yellow/Ochre,
   Light Yellow, Dark Yellow, Coral
   Pink, White
Masking tape
HB pencil
Ruler
Thick cardboard
Large sheet of white paper
Bucket

PREPARATION

See the embroidery design on the Pull
Out Pattern Sheet.

The painted design, ready for embroidery

STEP ONE

Make strong tea in the bucket with the tea bags and boiling water and add the vinegar. Place the fabric and the lace into the tea, swishing it around to get an even distribution of colour. Allow the fabric to dry, then press. Make sure the edges of the fabric are straight and the corners are square.

STEP TWO

Photocopy the design, then glue it to the large piece of paper. With the ruler and pencil, draw in the corner of the cloth, approximately 14 cm (5$^{1}/_{2}$ in) from the bottom of the pansy. Using masking tape, secure the design to a light box or a glass-topped table with a light underneath. Place the cloth on top so the design is in position on one corner. Trace the design onto the cloth, using the pencil. Repeat for each corner.

STEP THREE

Place the thick cardboard underneath the area to be coloured. Keeping the fabric firm and stable, apply the crayons lightly. Hold the crayon on the side of the point, stroking it in the same direction as the grain of the fabric, building up the colour gradually. To create the violet colour, alternate layers of Violet, Red and Blue crayon.

   Vary the greens by using Blue/Green, Yellow/Green, Yellow/Ochre, Light and Dark Yellow and Blue crayons. Enrich the yellow petals by combining layers of Light Yellow and Dark Yellow crayon and Coral Pink. To lighten a colour, add a layer of White crayon. Fix the crayon according to the manufacturer's instructions.

EMBROIDERY

Stitch the pansy spray, using stem stitch, back stitch, straight stitch and French knots, following the directions on the embroidery design and the illustration on page 28.

MAKING UP

STEP ONE

Turn under 4 mm (3/16 in) on the edges of the cloth. Press, then machine-stitch the hem. Attach the lace under the finished edge of the cloth, using a zigzag stitch.

STEP TWO

Machine-stitch one side of the bias binding to the lace. Cut the binding at each corner and overlap one end over the other, leaving 6 mm ($^{1}/_{4}$ in) at each corner. Turn under the 6 mm ($^{1}/_{4}$ in) allowance. Hand- or machine-stitch the other side of the bias binding into place.

Painted and embroidered pansies

Hand-painted Jugs from Victoria McCarthy, Roseville NSW; Silk Pansies from Hartshorne Design, Mosman NSW

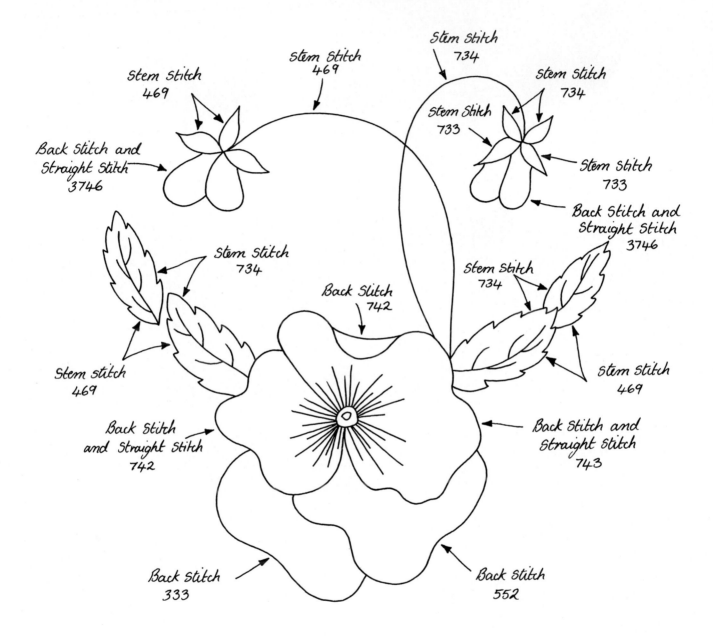

Stem Stitch
469

Stem Stitch
469

Stem stitch
734

Stem Stitch
733

Stem Stitch
734

Back Stitch and
Straight Stitch
3746

Stem Stitch
733

Back Stitch and
Straight Stitch
3746

Stem Stitch
734

Stem stitch
469

Stem Stitch
734

Back Stitch
742

Stem Stitch
469

Back Stitch
and Straight Stitch
742

Back Stitch and
Straight Stitch
743

Back Stitch
333

Back Stitch
552

Embroidery Design

TABLE MAT

By Laura Leverton

In pulled thread embroidery, such as this delicate table mat, the tension of the stitches changes the structure of the weave, creating the lacy effects on the petals and leaves.

MATERIALS

35 cm x 48 cm (14 in x 19 in) of 30-count linen
Four skeins of stranded cotton in a colour to match the linen
Bohin tapestry needle, size 26
Tracing paper
Water-soluble marker pen
Machine-sewing thread in a colour to match the linen
Fineline permanent marker pen

PREPARATION

See the embroidery design on page 30 and the Stitch Guide on pages 32-35.

STEP ONE

Fold a 1 cm (³/₈ in) double hem around the edges of the linen by counting twelve threads from the edge and making a fold on the thread line on the wrong side. Do this on all four sides of the linen. To mitre the corners, open out each corner of the linen and cut each corner as shown (Fig. 1). Refold the corner as indicated, exactly on the diagonal. Baste the hem and the corners. Stitch the mitred corners with invisible stitches, using the machine-sewing thread, then hemstitch the remaining hem.

STEP TWO

Using the permanent marker pen, trace the design, then pin it to the underside of the linen. Trace the design onto the linen, using small light dots with the water-soluble marker pen (or your favourite method of design transfer).

EMBROIDERY

STEP ONE

Embroider the outline and the stems, using whipped chain stitch for the outlines and palastrina stitch for the stems (see the Stitch Guide on pages 32-35).

STEP TWO

Following the diagram on page 30 and the Stitch Guide on pages 32-35, fill in the petals and the leaves in the stitches indicated. Start each of the filling stitches at the widest section of the space to be filled. This is done so as to see how the stitch forms. Once the edge is reached, turn the work around and work the next row.

Detail of embroidery

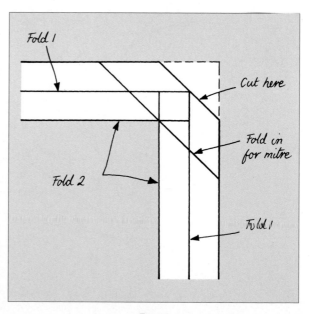

Fold 1

Cut here

Fold in for mitre

Fold 2

Fold 1

Fig. 1

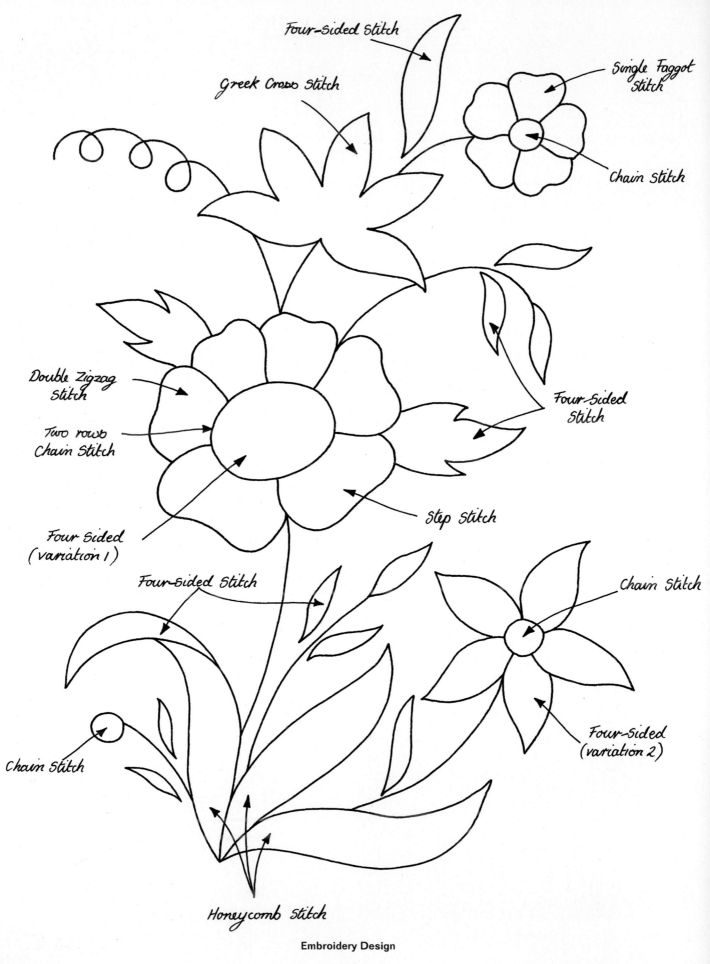

Four-sided Stitch

Greek Cross Stitch

Single Faggot Stitch

Chain Stitch

Double Zigzag Stitch

Two rows Chain Stitch

Four-sided Stitch

Four Sided (variation 1)

Step Stitch

Four-sided Stitch

Chain Stitch

Four-sided (variation 2)

Chain Stitch

Honeycomb Stitch

Embroidery Design

Plates, Cups and Saucers from Waterford Wedgwood, Castle Hill NSW; Cutlery from Stanley Rogers, Balmain NSW

STITCH GUIDE

WHIPPED CHAIN STITCH

Cover the design line with chain stitches, then whip them with another thread which is only anchored in the fabric at the beginning and the end of the work. Throughout, the needle is passed between the fabric and the chain stitch, so that the whipping stitch sits over the junction of each chain stitch (Fig. 2).

PALASTRINA STITCH

Working from left to right, using four strands of cotton, bring the needle up at **A** and make a small slanting stitch, inserting the needle at **B** and coming out at **C** (Fig. 3). Slide the needle between the thread and the fabric and gently pull the needle through (Fig. 4). Again, slide the needle between the thread and fabric, making a buttonhole loop (Fig. 5). Pull the thread gently. Make a small straight stitch to the right of the first stitch (Fig. 6). Repeat these four steps until the design outline is covered.

HONEYCOMB STITCH

Using two strands of cotton, work the stitch from right to left over two threads of linen, following steps **a** to **d**. Turn the work around to work the second row (Fig. 7).

SINGLE FAGGOT STITCH

This stitch is worked on the diagonal over three threads, using one strand of cotton. The stitches are straight on the right side of the fabric and diagonal on the wrong side. Each row is separated by one thread (Fig. 8).

GREEK CROSS STITCH

Using two strands of cotton, begin at step **a** by working a buttonhole stitch over three threads. Repeat the same process for steps **b** and **c**. Take the needle down at the centre as shown in step **d**. The final step closes around the thread where the stitch started. Work rows of the stitch on the diagonal separating each complete stitch from the next one by one thread as shown in step **e**. Leave one thread between each row (Fig. 9).

DOUBLE ZIGZAG STITCH

Work on the diagonal from right to left, using one strand of cotton. Following figure 10, work steps **a** to **d**. Work two rows over six threads, then two rows over three threads. Continue working two rows over six threads followed by two rows over three threads until the space is filled (Fig. 11).

STEP STITCH

This stitch is formed by working satin stitch blocks at right angles to each other. The stitch is made by combining four stitches over three threads (Fig. 12).

FOUR-SIDED STITCH

Work each stitch over two threads, using one strand of cotton and working steps **a** to **c** to form each stitch. Work the stitch from the right to left, forming a cross on the wrong side. Pull the stitch firmly (Figs 13, 14 and 15).

FOUR-SIDED STITCH VARIATION

Follow the formation of the four-sided stitch in figure 10, leaving one thread between each complete stitch (Fig. 16).

FOUR SIDED STITCH VARIATION

Follow the formation of the four-sided stitch in figure 11, leaving one thread between each complete stitch and each row (Fig. 17).

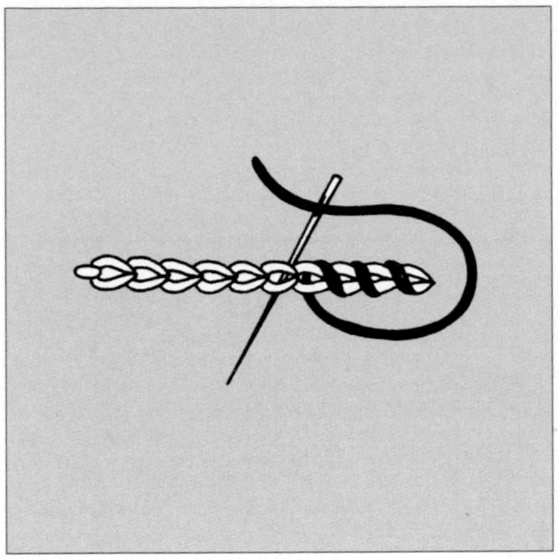

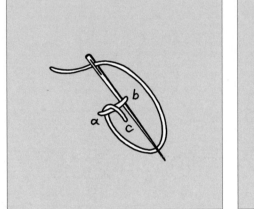

Fig. 2

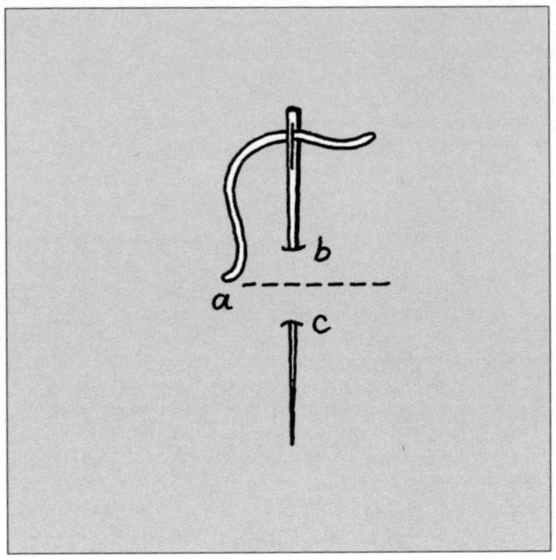

Fig. 3

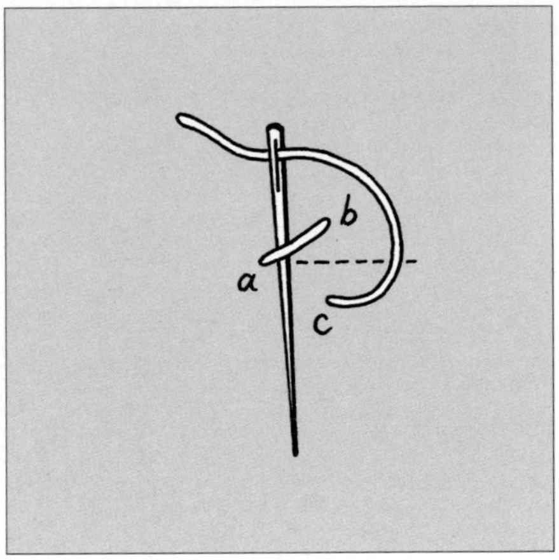

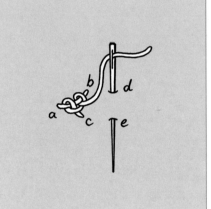

Fig. 4

Fig. 5

Fig. 6

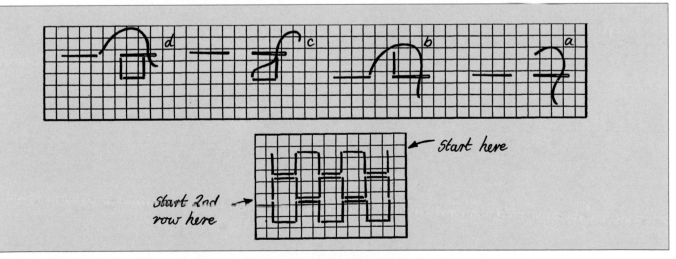

Fig. 7

33

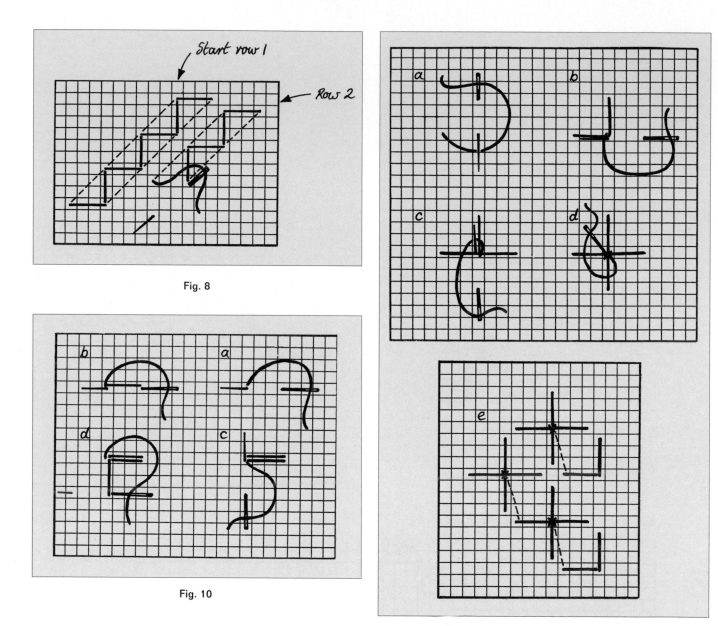

Fig. 8

Fig. 10

Fig. 9

34

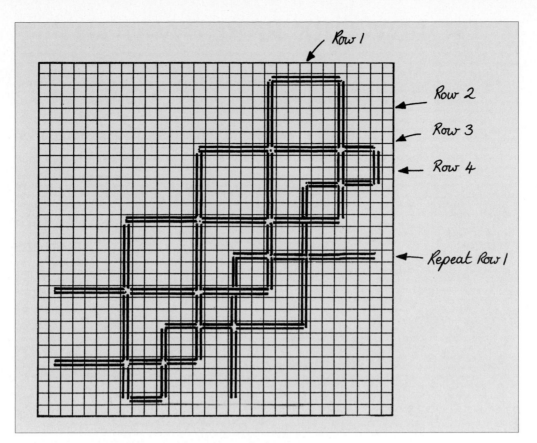

Row 1

Row 2

Row 3

Row 4

Repeat Row 1

Fig. 11

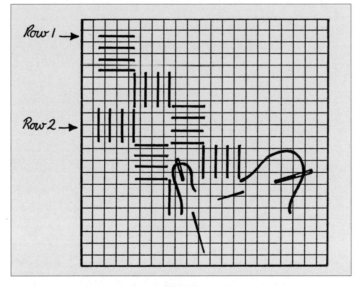

Row 1

Row 2

Fig. 12

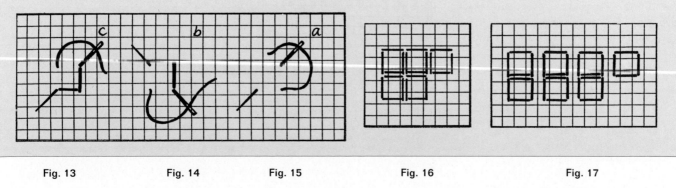

Fig. 13   Fig. 14   Fig. 15   Fig. 16   Fig. 17

GOLDWORK PAPERWEIGHT

By Janice Rawlinson

Embroidery with gold thread has a very long tradition. This elegant paperweight is an extension of that tradition with quite a contemporary look.

MATERIALS

Round clear glass paperweight, about 9 cm (3¹/₂ in) in diameter with a removable base

16 cm (6¹/₄ in) square of black fabric in a fairly fine weave

Piece of calico to suit the chosen frame

Madeira Twisted Thread Gold 9805-5012

Madeira Metallic Thread no. 12: Gold 34, Gold 33

Madeira Metallic Thread no. 40, Astro 1

Fine machine-sewing thread, Gold or Yellow Ochre, for couching

Rectangular tapestry frame or round frame

Tissue paper or nonwaxed lunchwrap

Fray stopper

Crewel needles, mixed sizes

Ordinary sewing cotton

Pencil

BEFORE YOU BEGIN

Goldwork or metallic thread embroidery is most easily worked when the background fabric is pulled taut in a frame. Although a rectangular frame is ideal, individual small embroideries are sometimes worked satisfactorily in a round frame.

It is always necessary to use two layers of fabric – calico is the ideal second layer.

PREPARATION

See the embroidery design on page 38.

STEP ONE

Pin and baste the black fabric to the calico. Position both layers of fabric into the round frame, or stitch and lace them into the rectangular frame. Tension the fabric on all sides.

STEP TWO

Using the pencil, trace the design onto the tissue paper or nonwaxed lunchwrap. Place the tracing onto the fabric and hold it in position with a pin in each corner.

STEP THREE

Baste along all the lines of the design, using a small running stitch, then carefully tear the paper away leaving the stitches to define the areas to be embroidered.

Fig. 1

EMBROIDERY

Note: Shapes **A**, **B** and **C** are filled in with metallic threads which are laid on the surface of the fabric and kept in place with simple couching, which is a small stab stitch placed across the metallic threads. Couching is necessary because most metallic threads are damaged when they are pulled through fabric, so they should be kept on the surface with only the ends taken through to the back. Shape **D** is filled with satin stitch.

STEP ONE

Start embroidering by filling the shape **A**. Release a small length of Gold twisted thread from its pack. Do not cut it. Thread the fine machine-sewing thread into a small crewel needle and couch the metallic thread to the fabric as shown in figure 1, being sure to leave a 6 cm (2³/₈ in) tail of Gold thread at the beginning which can be taken through to the back of the work later.

STEP TWO

Couch the metallic thread around the outline of the shape until you are back to where you started, then couch further rows inside the previously worked outline. When you are a little way past the starting point, take the 6 cm (2³/₈ in) tail of Gold thread to the back. Hold the tail in place on the back, using a couple of tiny stitches. Couch at least four rows of Gold thread, then cut it, taking care to leave a 6 cm (2³/₈ in) tail to take through to the back.

STEP THREE

Commence couching again, this time using the Madeira Metallic Thread no. 34. Start on the other edge of the ribbon shape and work towards its centre, eventually meeting up with the first four rows of the gold twisted thread. Fill each of the four loops **A** in the same manner.

STEP FOUR

The four **B** shapes are couched using Madeira Metallic Thread no. 33. Start at the outline and work towards the centre. You can allow the Gold thread to form tiny loops on the two outer corners.

STEP FIVE

Couch the four **C** shapes, using Madeira Metallic Thread no. 34. This time, instead of working from the outside to the centre of each shape, work from one side only. Continue this contour in all subsequent rows by turning the threads sharply back on themselves, and by laying each row close to the previous row. As an alternative, you can give the other side of these shapes an interesting outline by adding some fine braid or twisted cord, or maybe a row of chain stitch or loops, some tatting or even macramé.

STEP SIX

Work all the **D** segments in simple straight stitch or satin stitch, using Madeira Metallic Astro. Take care with the direction of these stitches and try to angle them into a neat tapered point.

MAKING UP

Take the embroidery out of the frame and cut it to size by drawing around the embroidery, using the template provided with the paperweight. Run a fine line of fray stopper around the edge of this fabric circle, then cut the embroidery neatly to size. Place the embroidery in the base of the paperweight. Peel the paper from the adhesive backing provided, then press this backing to the underside of the paperweight, enclosing the embroidery.

Embroidery Design

38

PAINTING WITH THREAD

By Valerie Craven

The concept of this project was to embroider the same design in several small pictures, using different-coloured threads and/or backgrounds to give a variety of effects.

MATERIALS

For each picture

12 cm x 15 cm (5 in x 6 in) pieces of light blue, yellow, dark blue, brown cotton or polycotton fabric

Piece of calico or simple backing fabric big enough to fit the embroidery frame

Embroidery frame, either a hoop at least 24 cm (9½ in) in diameter or rectangular

Small amounts of stranded cotton in suitable colours (this is a good opportunity to use up your scraps)

Tracing paper

Black fineline permanent marker pen

Pencil or fabric pen

Crewel needles

BEFORE YOU BEGIN

For each picture, choose a background colour which can be left free of embroidery for part of the picture. When determining the colour of thread to use for a particular area, it is important to be aware of the direction of the main source of light. It is helpful to put an arrow outside the picture to guide you.

PREPARATION

See the embroidery design on page 41.

STEP ONE

Using the marker pen, trace the design onto the tracing paper. To transfer the design to the fabric, tape the tracing to a window or a glass-topped table with a light source beneath. Place the fabric over the tracing and transfer the design lines, using the pencil or fabric pen.

STEP TWO

Attach the fabric with the traced design to the backing material, using straight stitch as shown below.

EMBROIDERY

Most of the picture is worked in straight stitch of different lengths using a single strand of embroidery cotton. Use French knots for foliage and other textures.

Note: Place all the starting and finishing knots outside the picture area, so they won't interfere with the needle. They will be hidden when the picture is stretched and mounted.

The work in progress

Detail pic no. 1

Detail pic no. 2

Detail pic no. 3

Detail pic no. 4

Embroidery Design

WARATAH BAG

By Margaret Browne

The inspiration for this project came from seeing the rare white waratah during a visit to the National Botanic Gardens in Canberra.

MATERIALS

Three pieces of fabric, each approximately 30 cm x 60 cm (12 in x 24 in) (one piece is the background fabric for the embroidery, the second piece is the backing or stabiliser and the third piece is for the lining)

Tapestry needles: sizes 24 and 16

Crewel needles

Fine sharp needle

2 m ($2^1/_4$ yd) of 4 mm ($^3/_{16}$ in) wide silk ribbon, Cream

2 m ($2^1/_4$ yd) of 7 mm ($^5/_{16}$ in) wide silk ribbon, Cream

1 m ($1^1/_8$ yd) of 4 mm ($^3/_{16}$ in) wide silk ribbon, Green

Ordinary sewing cotton to match the colour of the background fabric

Ordinary sewing cotton to contrast with the background fabric and embroidery threads

One skein of overdyed stranded cotton to match the Cream and Green ribbons, combined with a Gold blending filament

DMC Perle 8 thread: Pale Green 368, Medium Green 937

Embroidery frame, 20 cm (8 in) in diameter

Greaseproof paper

Black fineline permanent marker pen

5 cm (2 in) square of firm card

BEFORE YOU BEGIN

Take some care selecting the fabric for your bag. The one pictured is in green organza with a dark green silk backing fabric to enhance the Cream silk ribbons used for the embroidery. It has a paler green silk lining.

PREPARATION

See the embroidery design on the Pull Out Pattern Sheet.

STEP ONE

Press the fabric to remove any creases. Carefully baste together the edges of the background fabric and the stabiliser. Mark the centre of the fabric by finger-pressing it into quarters.

STEP TWO

Using the marker pen, trace the design onto the greaseproof paper. Place the tracing on the fabric then, using a basting stitch and the contrasting sewing cotton, outline the design on the fabric. These stitches can easily be removed while working the embroidery.

STEP THREE

Mount the background fabric, stabiliser and paper into the frame, making sure that the fabric is held as taut as possible without distorting it. Trace around the design with a sharp needle to perforate the greaseproof paper and then tear off all the paper.

EMBROIDERY

STEP ONE

Thread the large tapestry needle with approximately 28 cm (11 in) of 7 mm ($^5/_{16}$ in) wide Cream ribbon and the smaller tapestry needle with the same length of the overdyed cotton. Commence the embroidery at the centre front bottom row, using detached chain stitch, with the loop worked in the ribbon and the anchor stitch worked in the overdyed cotton. Work five rows, filling the centre area of the waratah. At the beginning and the end of each ribbon, take approximately 5 cm (2 in) of the ribbon to the back of the work. Sew this ribbon onto the stabiliser fabric, using the sharp needle threaded with the matching sewing cotton.

STEP TWO

Change to the 4 mm ($^3/_{16}$ in) wide Cream silk ribbon, threaded in the size 24 tapestry needle. Using detached chain stitch, fill the areas following the embroidery design. Thread approximately 28 cm (11 in) of the overdyed cotton onto a medium crewel needle and fill in the upper outer areas.

STEP THREE

Using a small tapestry needle and the Pale Green silk ribbon, work French knots to complete the top area of the waratah flower.

LEAVES

Using the sharp needle, and the Medium Green Perle 8 Cotton, outline the leaves in stem stitch then, using the Pale Green cotton, work two rows of stem stitch along the centre of the leaves.

MAKING UP

STEP ONE

Cut out the front and back of the bag, following the pattern provided. Carefully press the fabric around the embroidery, taking particular care not to iron the embroidered area.

STEP TWO

Baste the front and the back of the bag together, with the right sides facing. Stitch the side seams. Clip the curved seam allowances to allow them to sit flat, then press. Turn the bag right side out.

STEP THREE

Staystitch the raw top edges on the opening of the bag. Turn down the hem allowance and press again.

BAG LINING

STEP ONE

Cut out the lining, following the pattern provided. Machine-sew the seams, clip the curves, press. Staystitch the raw edges on the opening of the lining and turn down the hem, as for the bag.

STEP TWO

Slipstitch the lining to the bag at the top edge then, using the Pale Green Perle cotton, feather stitch the lining to the bag, taking care that the backs of the stitches do not show through.

CORDS

Measure the circumference of the bag, approximately 5 cm (2 in) from the top of the bag and multiply this by six. Knot together the ends of ten lengths of the Medium Green Perle Cotton, cut to this measurement. Pin the knot to a stationary object (an ironing board cover is good) and twist the strands together in a clockwise direction until they are twisted fairly tightly. Fold the length in half, holding the ends in one hand while you smooth out the cord as it twists, with the other hand. Tie a knot to keep the loose ends together.

TASSELS

STEP ONE

Wrap the Medium Green Perle Cotton fifty times around the card. Cut the thread. Thread a large tapestry needle with a 20 cm (8 in) length of Perle Cotton. Slide the needle under the thread at the top and pull the thread halfway through, then gently slip the wrapped threads off the card.

STEP TWO

Carefully separate half the threads at the top of the tassel only and nestle the end of the twisted cord in this area. Pull up the thread wrapped through the ends, then tie it in a knot.

STEP THREE

Wrap a 20 cm (8 in) length of thread firmly around the tassel, about 20 mm ($^3/_4$ in) from the top to divide the head from the skirt of the tassel. Tie a half knot, then turn it over and tie a reef knot. The ends of this thread can be mingled with the tassel by simply threading them into a large needle and taking them back down into the skirt of the tassel.

STEP FOUR

Thread a smaller tapestry needle with a long piece of thread which matches the tassel. Work detached buttonhole stitch, starting at the knot on the neck of the tassel. It may be necessary to increase and then decrease as you work up towards the neck of the tassel. Make a discreet French knot to finish, then take the remaining thread down through the tassel. Do not cut the ends at this stage.

STEP FIVE

Make a second twisted cord with a tassel, just like the first one.

STEP SIX

Place the twisted cords around the neck of the bag. Keep them in place by making a keeper, worked in bullion stitch, on each side of the seam and allow the tassels to fall between the keepers. Cut and trim the ends of the tassels to neaten them.

Keep the embroidery soft

Dainty tassels are a feature

PERFORATED PAPER PICTURE

By Helen Whelan

Flower pots in a window have a lovely country feel in this easy-to-stitch little picture.

Note: This little picture is an ideal way to use up your leftover threads. Create your own colour scheme to suit.

MATERIALS

Perforated paper or 14-count canvas (see Before You Begin for the size)
Variegated mohair, White/Pink/ Grey/Green
Stranded cotton, Ecru
Fine wool, Purple/Red
Variegated stranded cotton: Blue/ Green/Lilac, Green, Pinky Beige/ Yellow
Variegated Perle 5 Cotton, Pink/ Beige/Orange
Variegated fine wool, Purple
Perle 5 Cotton: Magenta, Grey
Tapestry needle, size 22 or 24

BEFORE YOU BEGIN

The picture is worked on perforated paper with a count of 14 threads to the inch. Canvas of similar count could be used – a slight difference in the size of the completed picture will result. The picture on paper measures 9 cm x 11 cm (3½ in x 4¼ in).

Perforated paper does not need to be stretched, so only three or four holes need to be left all around the embroidery. Canvas with 14 count will require about 5 cm (2 in) all round the finished piece. If you are working on canvas, work two rows of tent stitch all round the completed picture.

The spaces between the 'bricks' have been left bare, but tent stitch could be used to simulate mortar.

EMBROIDERY

See the embroidery graph and key on pages 48-49 and the Stitch Guide on page 46.

Note: Work all the embroidery, following the graph and key, beginning at the top of the graph.

STEP ONE

For the oblong crosses with the small crosses, work the long crosses first (**a-b**, **c-d**, **e-f**, **g-h**), then fill in the small crosses, stitching in the order indicated (Fig. 1).

STEP TWO

For the padded satin stitch, stitch from **1-2**, then cover with the stitches in the order indicated (Fig. 2).

STEP THREE

For the fly stitch, note that **1-2** is held in place by **3-4**. **1-2** does not go through the paper at the downward point. Work across the row, working **5-6**, held in place by **7-8**; **9-10**, held in place by **11-12** and so on (Fig. 3). When the row is completed, turn the work around and work back for the second row in the same manner.

STEP FOUR

For the cross stitch, work the stitches in the order indicated (Fig. 4).

STEP FIVE

For the composite stitch flowers, work the stitches in the order indicated (Fig. 5). Work **1-2**, a small straight stitch over one 'thread', then work two fly stitches, **3-4**, held in place by **5-6** (like **1-2**) and **7-8**, held in place by **9-10**. Note that **6** and **9** share the same hole. Using a furry, but fine thread, work stitches **1-21** as shown.

STEP SIX

For the leaf stitch, work the stitch in the order indicated (Fig. 6). A contrasting thread could be used for the vein **11-12**.

STEP SEVEN

For the tent stitch, work the stitch in the order indicated (Fig. 7).

STEP EIGHT

For the long tied crosses, work the crosses in the order indicated (Fig. 8). Complete and tie each cross as you go.

STEP NINE

Work a row of padded satin stitch as for step two.

STEP TEN

Work a rice stitch variation for the feet of the window box, working the stitches in the order indicated (Fig. 9).

STEP ELEVEN

Work two long straight diagonal stitches (**a-b** and **c-d**) with a Smyrna cross on top (Fig. 10). The vertical stitch of the Smyrna cross is stretched and the horizontal stitch is worked last of all.

STEP TWELVE

The diagonal boxes can be varied or all exactly the same – whichever you prefer (Fig. 11).

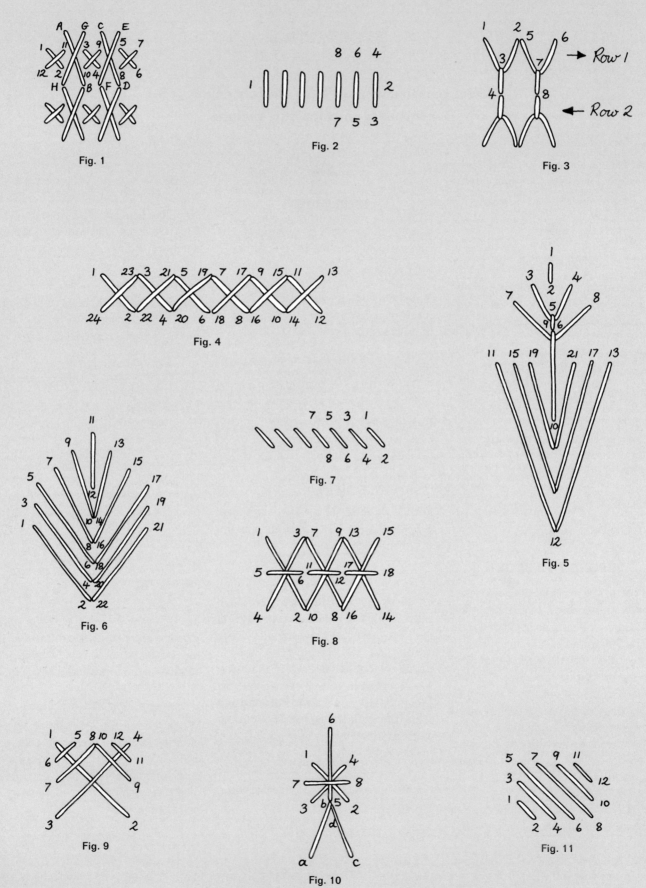

Fig. 1

Fig. 2

Fig. 3

Row 1

Row 2

Fig. 4

Fig. 5

Fig. 6

Fig. 7

Fig. 8

Fig. 9

Fig. 10

Fig. 11

COLOUR AND THREAD KEY

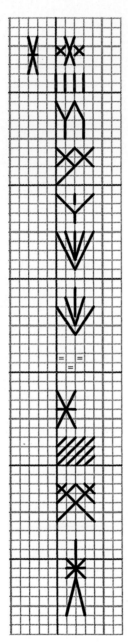

White/Pink/Grey/Green variegated mohair – oblong cross stitch with small cross stitch and long tied cross stitch

Ecru stranded cotton – padded satin stitch

Fine Purple/Red wool – fly stitch in two ways

Blue/Green/Lilac variegated stranded cotton – cross stitch

Pink/Beige/Orange variegated Perle 5 Cotton – fly stitch

Fine Purple variegated wool – long single stitches

Green variegated stranded cotton – leaf stitch

Magenta Perle 5 Cotton – tent stitch

Grey Perle 5 Cotton – long tied cross stitch

Pinky Beige/Yellow variegated stranded cotton – large diagonal stitch variation

Grey Perle 5 Cotton – rice stitch variation

Grey Perle 5 Cotton – composite stitch

Embroidery Graph

SNOW CRYSTALS CUSHION

By Effie Mitrofanis

Crisp blue fabric embellished with sparkling snow crystals and dainty tassels make this pretty pillow.

Finished size: 34 cm (13½ in) square

MATERIALS

Two 40 cm (16 in) squares of blue Dublin linen or Quaker cloth
One skein each of DMC Perle 3 Cotton: White, Ecru
One skein of DMC Soft Cotton, White
One ball or three skeins of DMC Perle 5 Cotton, Ecru
One ball DMC Perle 5 Cotton, White
One ball each of DMC Perle 8 Cotton, White, Ecru
Embroidery ribbon, White
One skein of DMC Stranded Cotton, White
Crewel needles in assorted sizes
5 cm (2 in) square of heavy cardboard
Cushion insert
Embroidery hoop or frame
Ordinary sewing cotton

PREPARATION

See the embroidery design on the Pull Out Pattern Sheet.

Overlock the edges of the linen squares. On one of the linen squares, baste in with the sewing cotton the dividing lines of the design and the six main arms of each of the snow crystals.

EMBROIDERY

Stitch the cushion, following the design. Use any of the listed threads to interpret the stitches and use different thicknesses in White or Ecru as suggested by the photograph or your own choices.

FOR THE LINES

Work the border lines in cable chain, working one row of cable chain with a row of stem stitch on either side for the thick lines.
SNOW CRYSTAL 1 (lower right-hand corner)
Work six fly stitches for the centre. Work the arms in stem stitch with bullion knots of twelve wraps each at the base. Work the leaves in back stitch.
SNOW CRYSTAL 2 (lower left-hand corner)
Work the centre as a spider's web with the arms in feather stitch. For the leaves, work detached chain stitch, using the embroidery ribbon.

Detail of one snow crystal

Detail of one snow crystal

SNOW CRYSTAL 3 (centre)

For the centre, work six long straight stitches alternated with six short straight stitches. Work the centre stars in detached chain stitch. Work the arms in stem stitch with the top of the arms and the spikes in straight stitch.

SNOW CRYSTAL 4 (top right)

Work the centre and part of the arms in detached chain stitch. For the rest of the arms use straight stitch with crossed double straight stitch at the top.

SNOW CRYSTAL 5 (top left)

For the centre work Cretan stitch, interlaced between two circles of back stitch (Fig. 1). For the long arms, use feather stitch; for the medium arms, use fly stitch with French knots, and for the short arms, use straight stitch with French knots.

TASSELS

Wrap Perle 5 Ecru around the card one hundred times. Tie the top of the tassel by threading 50 cm (19$\frac{1}{2}$ in) of the thread between the tassel and the card and tying it with a double knot. Remove the tassel from the card and wrap the neck with 1 m (1$\frac{1}{8}$ yd) of cotton. Finish off by threading the two ends, one at a time, into a needle and taking them down through the neck and blending them into the skirt of the tassel. Make four tassels in the same way.

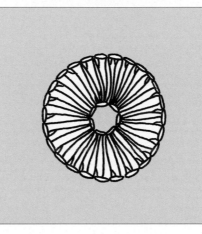

Fig. 1

MAKING UP

STEP ONE

Pin the front and back of the cushion with the right sides together. Machine-stitch around the edges, rounding the corners slightly and leaving an opening for turning. Trim the seams, turn the cushion right side out and press.

STEP TWO

Attach the tassels to the cushion cover by threading a needle with the two ends of the holding cord and stitching it through the cushion at the points indicated on the design. Work a buttonhole stitch at the top of each tassel, then take the thread ends down into the skirt of the tassel. Trim.

STEP THREE

Slip the cushion insert inside the cover. Slipstitch the opening closed.

COUNTERCHANGE SMOCKED BASKET

By Onita Pollitt

Counterchange smocking is worked on striped or checked fabric. A woven stripe gives best results, but more importantly, the stripes need to be even. This technique requires fabric that is twice the width of the finished size.

MATERIALS

Approximately 25 cm x 70 cm (10 in x 28 in) of suitable striped fabric for the lid
Approximately 1 m (1¹⁄₈ yd) of fabric for the lining
Firm cardboard
Wadding for the lid and the base of the basket
Craft glue
Approximately 7 m (7³⁄₄ yd) of lace edging (the exact length will depend on the size of your basket)
Bias binding
Basket with a hinged lid
Strong thread (Perle 8 Cotton is ideal, but four strands of stranded cotton can also be used)
Water-soluble marker pen
Ruler
Crewel needle, size 7

PREPARATION

Using the marker pen and ruler, draw lines on the right side of the fabric across the stripes. The distance between the lines should be equal to the width of the stripes.

COUNTERCHANGE SMOCKING

See the graph on page 56.

STEP ONE

Starting on a dark stripe, knot the thread and come through to the right side of the fabric at **A**, go down to **B** and take a small back stitch. Go across the stripe to **C**, take another stitch, go up the stripe, take a stitch at **D** (Fig. 1). Pull the thread so the fabric closes between **B** and **C**. Continue in this manner, taking a stitch at **E** and **F**, again pulling the thread to close the stripe at **E**. Remember, only pull the thread on the vertical stitches.

STEP TWO

Continue across the desired width, finishing on a dark stripe. Take the thread to the back of the fabric and tie it off. Complete two more rows in the same manner, following the graph.

STEP THREE

Leaving a space to suit the size of your lid, complete three more rows of trellis counterchange on rows 7-12.

MAKING UP

STEP ONE

Cut the cardboard to fit the size of the basket lid. Cut the wadding to the same shape. Glue the wadding to the cardboard.

STEP TWO

Fold the fabric between rows 2 and 3 and 10 and 11. Glue the smocked piece to the wadding/cardboard.

Counterchange smocking utilises the stripe of the fabric

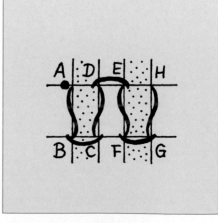

Fig. 1

Gather the lace to fit around the cardboard piece. Join the ends with a small seam to form a loop. Glue the lace under the edge of the cardboard, then glue the whole piece to the lid of the basket.

LINING

STEP ONE

Measure the side of the basket from the base up the side and over the rim. To this measurement, add approximately 10 cm (4 in) for seam allowances. This is the depth. Measure around the rim of the basket and add half this measurement again for fullness. This is the length. Cut two pieces of fabric, each this depth and half the length.

STEP TWO

Join the short ends of the fabric pieces to make a loop, leaving openings on top at the halfway marks deep enough to bring the fabric around the handles.

STEP THREE

Turn under the raw edge at the top edge, then sew the bias binding on the wrong side, over the raw edge to make a casing for the elastic.

STEP FOUR

Whip the lace to the finished top edge. At the bottom edge, stitch two rows of gathering.

STEP FIVE

Fit the fabric into the basket and around the handles. Thread the elastic through the casing and pull it up to fit the basket snugly. Join the ends of the elastic. Pull up the gathering threads at the bottom, tie them off, then glue the gathered fabric to the base of the basket.

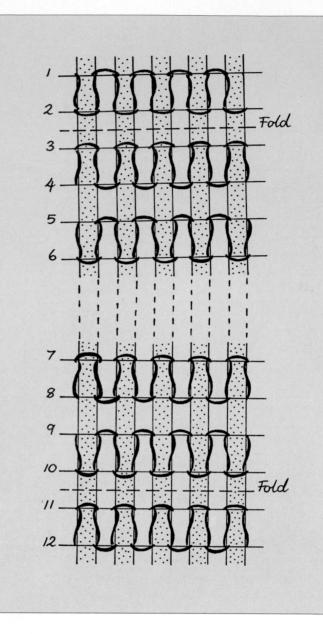

STEP SIX

Place the basket onto a sheet of cardboard and trace the shape of the base. Trim this shape slightly so it fits inside the basket. Glue a piece of wadding to one side of the cardboard, then place the cardboard (wadding side down) on a piece of fabric. Cut out the fabric, allowing an extra 1.5 cm (⅝ in) for turning. Fold this allowance over the edge of the cardboard and glue it in place. Run lines of glue across cardboard, then press it into the base of the basket, over the gathered fabric.

LANDSCAPE

By Jean Herring

A holiday snapshot of a hillside dotted with trees and native grasses was the inspiration for this embroidered landscape.

Note: The instructions given here are for embroidering this particular picture. If you wish to take your own photograph and embroider that, use these instructions as a guide. This is a project for which some embroidery experience is helpful.

MATERIALS

30 cm x 40 cm (12 in x 16 in) of calico
15 cm x 30 cm (6 in x 12 in) each of
   medium blue and dark blue cotton
   or polycotton fabric (no heavier
   than homespun)
30 cm (12 in) square of cinnamon
   cotton or polycotton fabric (no
   heavier than homespun)
30 cm x 40 cm (12 in x 16 in) of
   off-white silk organza
DMC Stranded Cotton: 372, 435, 451,
   453, 520, 677, 729, 733, 743, 801,
   924, 926, 927, 936, 937, 975, 3011,
   3022, 3072, 3363, 3781, 3790
22 cm x 32 cm (8⅝ in x 12½ in) flat
   frame (inside measurements)
Basting thread

Crewel needles, sizes 9 and 10
Two G clamps
Small pieces of felt
Pencil
Tracing paper (optional)
Sheet of paper, A3 size

PREPARATION

See the pattern on the Pull Out Pattern Sheet and the embroidery design on page 58.

STEP ONE

Attach the calico to the frame as tightly as possible – it may be necessary to turn the edges under to fit the frame. Clamp the frame to the edge of a table, leaving both hands free for working. Use pieces of felt under the clamps to protect the table.

STEP TWO

Trace the pattern pieces and markings directly onto the fabrics and cut them out – no seam allowance is needed. If you find it difficult to trace directly onto the fabric, use tracing paper. Place the fabric pieces onto the calico matching all the markings. Place the organza on top (Fig. 1).

STEP THREE

Cut a 15 cm x 23 cm (6 in x 9 in) window in the sheet of paper. Place the window on top of the fabrics, centring it carefully. Using small stitches, baste around the edge of the window. This will hold the fabrics in place and mark the edge of the embroidery. Remove the paper.

EMBROIDERY

STEP ONE

Using one strand of 3022, back stitch through all layers, close to the cut edges of the fabric (Fig. 2).

STEP TWO

Using the embroidery design as a guide, embroider the details of the landscape in the colours and stitches indicated. Do not mark the designs on the organza, but work freehand.

STEP THREE

For the spinifex, work in straight stitch, using one strand of 372. Work over this with straight stitch in one strand of 677. Work in fly stitch, using one strand of 729 over the top of the straight stitch.

STEP FOUR

For the stones, work French knots in two strands of the appropriate colours, scattering groups of each colour until the space is filled.

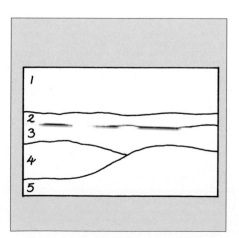

Fig. 1

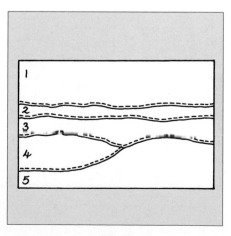

Fig. 2

STEP FIVE

For the tree trunks, work rows of stem stitch until the trunk is large enough. Small trees will need only one row. For the leaves on the large trees, work in detached chain stitch, using one strand of thread in each colour separately to look like leaves. For the small trees, work French knots with two strands.

STEP SIX

For the wattle ground cover, use detached chain stitch in two strands for the greenery, placing the larger stitches in the front.

STEP SEVEN

For the flowers, work in bullion stitch using one strand of thread, ten to twelve wraps in the front and five to six wraps in the middle. Work French knots at the back.

KEY

STITCHES

A Straight stitch
B Fly stitch
C French knot
D Stem stitch
E Detached chain
F Bullion stitch

THREADS

0	3022
1	372
2	677
3	729
4	3781
5	801
6	975
7	435
8	927
9	3790
10	451
11	937
12	3363
13	936
14	733
15	926
16	924
17	3011
18	3072
19	520
20	743
21	453

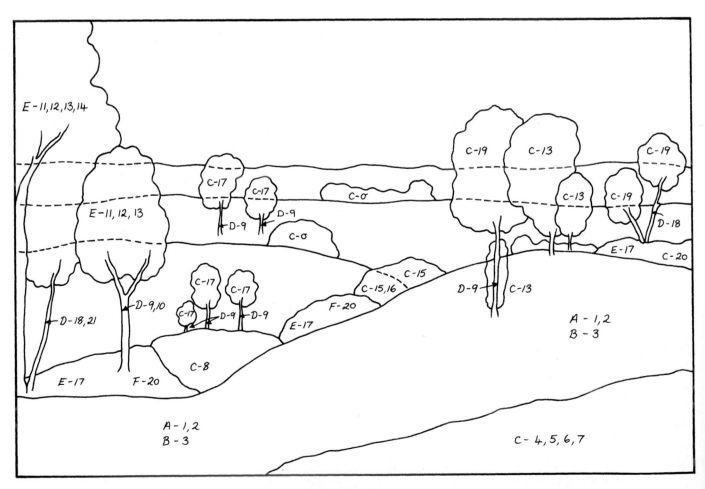

Embroidery Design

CANDLEWICK CUSHION

By Onita Pollitt

Using traditional candlewicking stitches in decidedly non-traditional colours, this cushion has great appeal.

Finished size: approximately 40 cm (16 in) square

MATERIALS

Approximately 130 cm x 150 cm (50 in x 60 in) of calico or homespun
Small amount of contrasting fabric for the piping
165 cm (65 in) of piping cord
DMC Perle 8 Cotton, Green 369
DMC Perle 5 Cotton, Green 369, Cream 746
DMC Perle 3 Cotton: Pale Pink 605, Medium Pink 3687
Crewel needles, sizes 3, 5, 7
50 cm (20 in) square of thin wadding
40 cm (16 in) cushion insert
Water-soluble marker pen
Black fineline permanent marker pen
Tracing paper
Masking tape
Embroidery hoop

PREPARATION

See the pattern on the Pull Out Pattern Sheet.

Cut three 50 cm (20 in) square pieces from the calico. Transfer the design onto one of these pieces, taking care to centre the design on the fabric. The simplest way to do this is to trace the design from the pattern sheet, using the marker pen. Tape the tracing to a window or to a glass-topped table with a light underneath and place one square of the calico over the top. Trace over the design, using the water-soluble marker pen. Place the fabric with the tracing in the hoop, making sure it is held quite taut.

EMBROIDERY

Embroider the design, using the size 3 crewel needle for the Perle 3 Cotton, the size 5 crewel needle for the Perle 5 Cotton and the size 7 crewel needle for the Perle 8 Cotton. Work the stitches marked on the pattern.

MAKING UP

STEP ONE

Baste the wadding, then a second square of calico, to the back of the embroidered square.

STEP TWO

Cut 3 cm (1¼ in) wide bias strips from the contrasting fabric. Join them together to form a strip 165 cm (65 in) long. Fold the strip over double with the wrong sides together and the piping cord sandwiched in between.

Using the zipper foot on the sewing machine, sew the cord inside the bias strip. Pin, then stitch the piping around the right side of the cushion front.

STEP THREE

Cut 3.2 m (3½ yd) of 22 cm (8½ in) wide calico for the ruffle. You will need to join pieces to achieve this length. Join the short ends to form a loop. Fold the loop over double with the raw edges even. Gather the raw edges as one. Pin the ruffle around the right side of the cushion front, adjusting the gathers and placing a little extra fullness at the corners. Stitch the ruffle in place, stitching in the piping stitching line.

STEP FOUR

Place the cushion front and back together, with the right sides facing and the raw edges even. Stitch around three sides. Turn the cover right side out, slip the insert inside and slipstitch the opening closed.

A simple design is enhanced by the use of colour

CARING FOR YOUR EMBROIDERY

Heather Joynes

Heather is a tutor with the Embroiderers' Guild and the author of several books. She has a particular interest in the history of embroidery and its conservation.

Always press embroidery on the wrong side on a well-padded surface, such as a folded towel.

CLEANING

Use simple methods first; fragile textiles need a gentle touch. Wash them carefully by hand, never by machine. A piece of plastic flyscreen is a useful aid. Lay the embroidery on the flyscreen and lower it into the water. The fabric will cling to the mesh so there is no stress on the fibres.

Use only lukewarm water at first. If this doesn't work, dissolve a small amount of Softly or Lux Flakes and try that.

Don't use strong pre-wash soakers on fragile textiles.

Rinse thoroughly and often. Use distilled or filtered water (from the chemist, not the service station) for the final rinse.

DRYING

Dry embroidery away from light and heat. Reverse the flyscreen and flick the article onto a thick towel. Gently roll up the towel. This will be sufficient to dry small items. Larger items will dry more quickly if a hair dryer on a low-heat setting is used, but take care to hold it away from the fabric. Don't iron fragile items, such as lace, but pin them out on a polystyrene board, covered with a towel (using lace pins) until they are dry.

STORING

Oven bags are convenient for storing small articles – never use plastic bags. Store pieces flat.

Cover a cardboard roll with lawn or sheeting, then roll runners, tray cloths, tablecloths on this, securing them with two or three tapes tied loosely around the roll.

Rather than acid-free tissue paper, small items can be stored in sheeting bags.

WALLHANGINGS

Wallhangings should be mounted on acid-free card, padded with thin Pellon wadding. Never spray them with Scotchguard. If you are concerned about dust, vacuum the piece lightly, but first protect the piece by covering the nozzle of the vacuum cleaner with two layers of net.

If the piece is to be framed under glass, a spacer of acid-free material should be placed between the embroidery and the glass.

Avoid strong light – artificial, as well as sunlight.

If possible, wedding dresses and christening robes should be stored flat in an acid-free box. If that is not possible, stitch loops of tapes at the inside waist, turn the garment inside out and hang it from the loops on a well-padded hanger. A bag of sheeting, open at the bottom, which fits over the hanger will give additional protection. Net or tulle can be used to fill out sleeves, bonnets etc.

TABLE LINEN

Store doilies flat in acid-free folders.

Do not press tablecloths until you are ready to use them. Don't store starched articles – they will attract silverfish and moths. To protect against these pests, inspect the garments regularly and give them an occasional airing (away from the light).

BEADED DRESSES

Beaded items should be stored flat on a lifting sheet. Do not hang them, as the beading stresses the fabric, especially at the shoulders.

BEADED BLACKWORK

By Rosie Ansley

You can make eight different decorations by varying the threads and background fabrics. These designs are all suitable for the beginner.

MATERIALS

For each piece

10 cm (4 in) square of 18 count black or white Aida fabric

DMC Perle 8 Cotton thread, Black or White

6 cm (2³⁄₈ in) round gold frame

Nine small gold beads

6 cm (2³⁄₈ in) diameter circle of thin wadding (optional)

Embroidery thread, Gold

Embroidery scissors

Tapestry needle, size 24

BEFORE YOU BEGIN

Blackwork designs are worked in double running stitch, also called Holbein stitch. The back of the work should appear the same as the front. This means you can't carry threads across the back of the work where they may show through the fabric and spoil the look of the final design.

EMBROIDERY

See the embroidery graphs on page 66.

STEP ONE

Find the centre of the Aida fabric square by folding the fabric into quarters and finger-pressing the folds. This point corresponds to the centre of the design.

STEP TWO

Start at the centre of the design, leaving a sufficiently long thread on the back of the work to weave behind your completed stitching. Work a row of running stich in one direction (Fig. 1), working each stitch over two threads of the fabric.

STEP THREE

Work back along the design line filling in the missing stitches on the return journey (Fig. 2). The heavier shading indicates the return journey stitches.

STEP FOUR

Finish by weaving the beginnings and ends of thread under previously completed stitching on the back of the work.

BEADING

Using the Gold thread, attach a gold bead at each small circle marked on the graph. Run the Gold thread under the back of the stitching, bringing the needle up where the bead is to be placed. Thread the bead onto the needle and take the needle down through the fabric. Run the Gold thread under the completed stitching to where the next bead is to be placed and repeat the process.

MAKING UP

Use the plastic back of the frame to draw the circle of wadding, if you wish to pad your design. Place the embroidery, wadding and plastic back into the frame. Check that the embroidery is properly centred, before using the embroidery scissors to trim away any excess fabric close to the back of the frame.

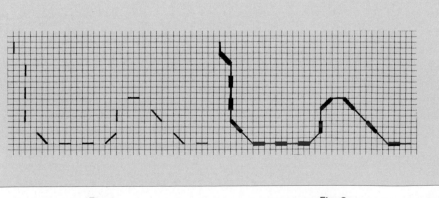

Fig. 1   Fig. 2

Embroidery Graphs

EMBROIDERED BLOUSE

By Janet Luce

A simple design of pulled threads and tiny embroidered flowers, makes this elegant fine linen blouse.

MATERIALS

Any simple round-necked short-sleeved blouse pattern
One reel of Mettler Embroidery Thread Art 240 in a colour to match the fabric
Tapestry needles, size 26
Sufficient fabric
One skein of stranded cotton
Crewel needles, size 10
Tracing paper
Black fineline permanent marker pen
Sharp pencil
Stiletto

PREPARATION

See the embroidery design on the Pull Out Pattern Sheet.

Note: The embroidery is worked on the fabric before the blouse is cut out.

STEP ONE

Cut a rectangle of fabric about 5 cm (2 in) bigger all around than is needed for the blouse front. Finger-crease the piece into quarters to find the centre.

STEP TWO

Measure 1.75 cm (³/₄ in) on either side of the centre front. Beginning at the top, pull one thread the length of the design so the pulled thread is loose at the bottom of the design. Leave this thread at the back of the fabric – it will be worked into the stitching later. Leave the next four threads, then pull another thread to the same length as the first one.

EMBROIDERY

STEP ONE

Using the two lines of pulled threads as a guide, begin working four-sided stitch down the length of the design,
using the Mettler Embroidery Thread in the size 26 tapestry needle (Figs. 1-7). Approximately 1 cm (³/₈ in) from the desired length, hold the two drawn threads behind the fabric so they are caught into the back of the stitching to secure them.

STEP TWO

To turn the corner at the bottom of the square, draw two more threads as before, but this time draw them across the fabric and four threads apart. To do this, mark the length of the crossbar. Using a needle, pull up the thread in the centre and cut it, so that you can draw the two ends back. Be careful to draw the threads only to the measurement you need. Stitch the drawn threads into the back of the stitching as before.

STEP THREE

When you have worked the four-sided stitch across the bottom, pull another two vertical threads as before and work up the other side.

Four-sided stitch gives a delicate finish on linen

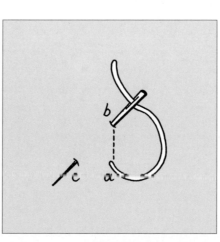

Fig. 1

You can embroider a fabric-covered button to complete the effect

STEP FOUR

Measure and mark the positions of the other crossbars. Pull the threads and work the crossbars in four-sided stitch to form the squares.

STEP FIVE

For the flowers, trace the flower motif onto tracing paper, using the marker pen. Place the tracing under the fabric in the centre of every second square and trace in the flower very, very lightly with the pencil. Be sure to cover these lines with the stitching. Using one strand of the Stranded Cotton, outline the centre eyelet in one row of running stitch, then turn and work back, filling in the spaces (Holbein stitch). Pierce the centre of each flower with the stiletto and overcast the eyelet.

STEP SIX

Using one strand of the Stranded Cotton, work ten satin stitches lengthwise on each petal for padding, then work more satin stitches over the top.

SLEEVES

Work out how far down the sleeve you want the design to finish. Cut each piece of the fabric 5 cm (2 in) bigger all around than the sleeve. Work the embroidery in the same way as for the front, then cut out the sleeves.

BACK

When cutting out the blouse back, allow sufficient fabric at the centre

back to fold over three times. This way you will not need to use interfacing. Make the hem by folding back the fabric twice. Baste the hem, then pin stitch down both sides.

BUTTONS

Embroider a small flower on small scraps of the fabric, then use these scraps to cover the buttons.

MAKING UP

Make up the blouse, following the instructions in the pattern packet. For such fine linen it is best to use French seams and to bind the neck and sleeves with self-fabric bias binding.

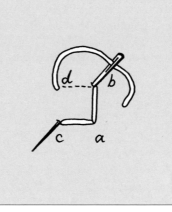

Fig. 2

Fig. 3

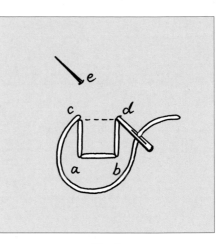

Fig. 4

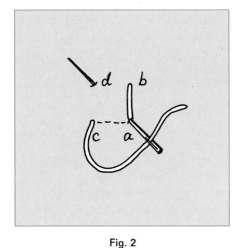

Fig. 5

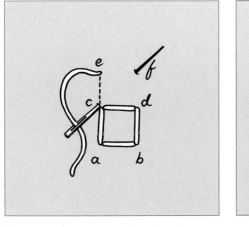

Fig. 6

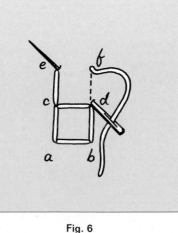

Fig. 7

MACRAME TASSEL

By Barbara Curran

This is an elegant, medium-sized tassel which is very suitable for bell pulls, wallhangings, evening bags, bookmarks and the handles of furniture. The tassel can be attached to any item either by sewing it on or by using a lark's head knot.

MATERIALS

Two balls of DMC Perle 8 Cotton
10 cm x 15 cm (4 in x 6 in) of heavy cardboard or something similar

HANGING CORD

Cut six lengths of thread, each 150 cm (60 in). Knot them together at one end. Attach this end to a firm surface and twist until the whole length is firmly twisted. Fold this in half to form a twisted cord. Knot the ends together. Fold in half again. Knot the ends together again, forming a loop.

TASSEL

STEP ONE

Wrap the cotton two hundred times around the 15 cm (6 in) side of the cardboard. Cut through the cotton along one edge only and remove it from the cardboard. Lay the cotton flat on a table.

STEP TWO

Place the knot of the looped, twisted cord 10 cm (4 in) from one of the cut edges of the tassel skirt, facing toward the short end of the tassel skirt. Using a piece of Perle Cotton, tie the skirt to the looped cord, gathering the skirt thread evenly around the cord to enclose the knot (Fig 1). Wrap them both together two or three times, then tie off firmly

with a reef knot. Make sure that the knot is evenly covered with the loose cotton threads.

STEP THREE

Hold the tassel by the looped cord so the longer cords of the skirt hang over the shorter cords. Wrap a separate piece of Perle Cotton around the neck 1 cm (3/8 in) from the top of the head and above the knot (Fig. 2). Tie off the wrap as shown in figures 3 and 4.

STEP FOUR

With the longer ends of the skirt, tie seven rows of alternating square knots, using four threads for each knot and making eleven knots in each row (Figs 5 and 6).

STEP FIVE

Tie one row of alternating overhand knots (Fig. 7). Trim the ends of the skirt.

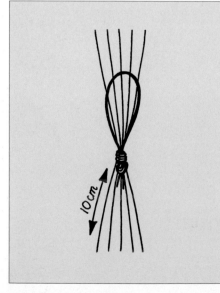

Fig. 1

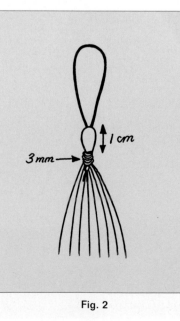

Fig. 2

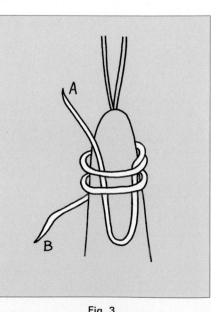

Fig. 3

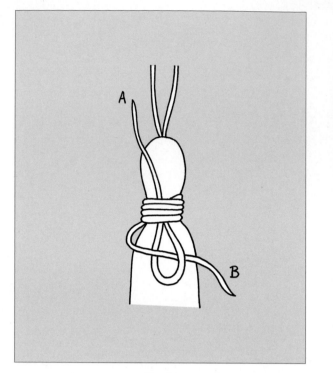

Fig. 4

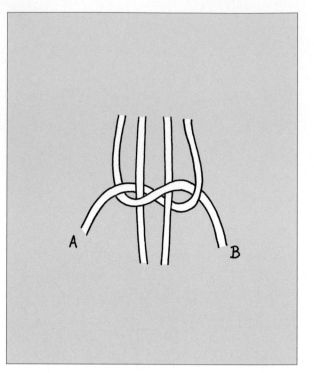

Fig. 5

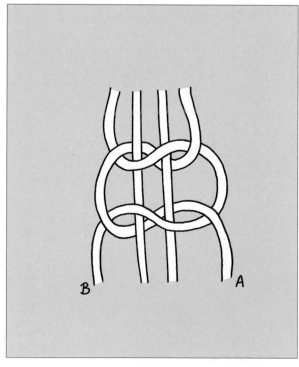

Fig. 6

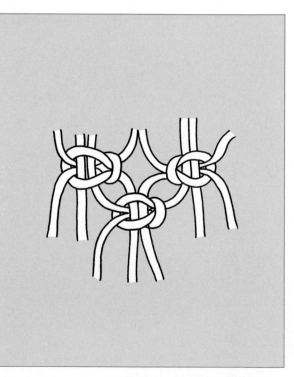

Fig. 7

NATURAL FIBRE TASSEL

By Barbara Curran

This is a very full, flamboyant tassel. It uses natural fibres which go so well with the 'country' look of today. The tassel is a little more difficult to make than some other tassels, but it is well worth the effort.

MATERIALS

One ball of knitting cotton
One hank of 16/2 linen thread, unbleached
Wood tassel mould, any shape, approximately 7 cm high x 4 cm wide (2³/₄ in high x 1¹/₂ in wide)
4 m (4¹/₂ yd) of fine fuse wire
Spray adhesive
Craft glue
Knitting needle, 6.5 mm
15 cm x 20 cm (6 in x 8 in) heavy cardboard or something similar
Pen or pencil

HANGING CORD

STEP ONE

Cut six 2 m (2¹/₄ yd) lengths each of the cotton and the linen thread. Fold both the cotton and linen threads in half,

then loop them together as shown in figure 1. Make a twisted cord as described on page 70.

STEP TWO

Cut a further four lengths of linen thread, each 2 m (2¹/₄ yd) long. Fold them in half and loop them through one end of the two-toned, twisted cord as shown in figure 2.

STEP THREE

Make the cords formed in steps one and two into a twisted cord. When you have finished, the new twisted cord will be three-toned.

TASSEL

STEP ONE

Spray the tassel mould with the spray adhesive. Wrap the linen thread around the tassel mould until it is

completely covered. Place a pen or a pencil into the centre hole of the tassel mould to assist with turning the mould while wrapping on the linen thread. Allow the adhesive to dry.

STEP TWO

Pull the twisted cord through the centre hole of the tassel mould. Using an over-hand knot, tie the two ends of the cord together at the bottom of the tassel mould. Cut the ends close to the knot and dab them with a little craft glue.

STEP THREE

Wind the knitting cotton thirty times around the 15 cm (6 in) side of the cardboard. Repeat this step until you have enough groups of wound cotton to go around the neck of your tassel mould. Leave a space between each group of thirty wraps and carry the knitting cotton from one group to the next. It is not necessary to cut the knitting cotton between groups.

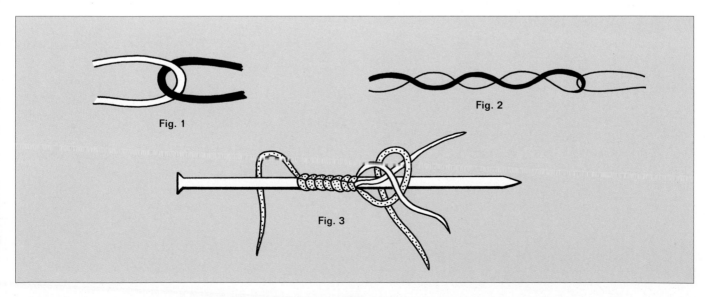

Fig. 1

Fig. 2

Fig. 3

Cut a piece of fuse wire 150 cm (60 in) long. Fold the fuse wire in half. Starting with the first group of thirty wraps, put one half of the fuse wire underneath the group, at the top. Place the second half of the fuse wire over the group and then twist both pieces of fuse wire together in an anticlockwise direction. Repeat this step with the next group of wraps, until all the wrapping groups are joined together with the fuse wire. At the opposite edge to where the fuse wire has been attached, cut through the bottom edge of each wrapping group to free them from the cardboard.

Attach the tassel skirt firmly to the neck of the tassel head by twisting the fuse wire ends together. Cut off any surplus at the ends of the fuse wire. If the skirt is too long, cut off any surplus wrapping groups at this time. Flatten the twisted fuse wire ends against the neck of the tassel head.

NECK RUFF

STEP ONE

Cut a piece of fuse wire 2 m ($2^{1}/_{4}$ yd) long. Fold it in half. Wind knitting cotton once around the knitting needle, then twist the fuse wire around the loop of the knitting cotton in an anticlockwise direction (Fig 3). Repeat this step until the work is two to three times longer than the neck of the tassel head.

Remove the ruff from the knitting needle and wrap it firmly around the neck of the tassel head a number of times. Secure by twisting the ends of the fuse wire together. Cut off the surplus fuse wire and bury the ends in the neck ruff.

TO COMPLETE

Trim the ends of the skirt by cutting it so that it is 13-14 cm (5-5$^{1}/_{2}$ in) long. Comb the skirt with a wide tooth comb for a good finish.

EQUIPMENT

SCISSORS

A good pair of embroidery scissors with fine sharp points is essential. They should not be used for any other purpose – have another pair of larger scissors for cutting fabric and a heavy-duty pair for cutting paper. Keep your embroidery scissors in a protective holder when they are not in use.

NEEDLES

It is important to match needles, fabric and thread. Bear in mind that the needle creates a passage in the fabric for the thread to follow; the thicker the thread, the thicker should be the needle. The most commonly used needles for embroidery are:

Crewel needles come in various sizes, have a fairly long eye and a sharp point. They are suitable for crewel work and other surface stitchery.

Tapestry needles have a large eye and a ball point. They are used for embroidery on canvas and evenweave fabrics as the ball point slips between the fabric threads without breaking them.

Chenille needles come in various sizes, have a large eye and a sharp point. They are ideal for thicker threads such as ribbon and wool, and for knotted stitches.

Straw needles are long needles with a small round eye and a sharp point. They are also called milliners' needles. The long shank makes them most suitable for bullion stitch.

Betweens are short stubby needles with a round eye and a sharp point. Traditionally used by tailors, they are good for quick, even stitching on heavy fabric or for quilting.

Beading needles are very fine and long with slim eyes and are especially made for threading beads and pearls.

Leather needles have triangular points that pierce without tearing. They can also be used on vinyl and plastic.

Easy threading needles have a slot eye into which the thread is drawn. They are ideal for those who have trouble threading ordinary needles.

Other needles are darners, bodkins for lacing and threading, curved needles for upholstery, sharps for general sewing and machine-sewing needles.

THREADS

Tapestry wool is a 4-ply nondivisible yarn which comes in a wide range of colours and is used for canvas work and creative embroidery.

Crewel wool usually comes in three 2-ply strands and has a loose twist.

Fine crewel wool is a fine single strand wool, used for crewel work.

Stranded cotton comes in skeins of six strands to be used in any multiples. Always separate strands before using them. Stranded cotton also comes in hand-dyed variations.

Perle cotton comes in four weights: 3, 5, 8 and 12. The thread has a distinctive twist which makes it appear shiny. It is also available in hand-dyed variations.

Broder is a tightly twisted, unmercerised yarn which is available in several weights.

Flower thread is a very fine single strand thread with a matte finish.

Silk is a soft thread with a satin sheen. It is also available in hand-dyed variations.

Rayon is a very shiny thread, but is not as easy to manipulate as silk.

Metallic threads come in gold and silver, as well as many novelty metallic threads. Fine metallic threads, blending filaments, can be mixed with other threads.

Other threads available are linen threads, cotton threads made especially for candlewicking, and a variety of novelty threads, such as bouclé and ribbon. For creative embroidery, some knitting and crochet cottons are also used.

FABRICS

Mono interlock canvas has single vertical and horizontal threads twisted at the junctions. The junctions should not move during stitching.

Mono interwoven canvas has single vertical and horizontal threads woven at the junctions, allowing the junctions to be moved during stitching to create holes and a lacy effect.

Penelope (double mesh) canvas has pairs of vertical and horizontal threads. It is a strong canvas which takes diagonal stitches better than straight stitches.

Canvas comes in a variety of thread counts from very fine to very coarse. All canvas contains size to give it a crisp smooth surface, preventing wear on the thread. Canvas should be worked on a frame as handling breaks down the size, softening it, thus affecting the tension and placement of the stitches.

Evenweave linen has single vertical and horizontal threads woven with the same number of warp threads and weft threads per centimetre (inch). It comes in several thread counts and colours. Evenweave fabrics also come in cottons and mixtures, and the various thicknesses of the fabric threads suit different stitch techniques.

Aida cloth has groups of threads woven to form squares with the same number of warp and weft threads per centimetre (inch). Made of cotton, it comes in several thread counts and colours and is easy to stitch.

Other fabrics are also used, including many fabrics that are not especially made for embroidery.

STITCH GUIDE

CHAIN STITCH

Chain stitches can be worked singly or in a row.

To begin, bring the needle through from the back of the fabric. Reinsert the needle very close beside where it first emerged, leaving a loop.

Bring the needle out again one stitch length away, so the the loop lies beneath the point of the needle. Gently pull the stitch taut.

Continue making stitches this way.

For a twisted chain stitch, instead of reinserting the needle just beside where it first emerged, insert the needle so that the ribbon, cotton or wool crosses over at this point.

WHIPPED CHAIN STITCH

Cover the design line with chain stitch, then whip them with another thread which is only anchored in the fabric at the beginning and the end of the work. Throughout, the needle is passed between the fabric and the chain stitch, so that the whipping stitch sits over the junction of each chain stitch.

DETACHED CHAIN STITCH

Bring the needle up through the fabric at the point where you wish the stitch to sit. Work a single chain stitch, taking the needle to the back of the work at the end of the anchor stitch.

PISTIL STITCH

Work a straight stitch. Work a French knot at one end of the straight stitch.

BULLION STITCH

Bullion stitches are used either on their own or in groups to create roses.

To make a bullion stitch, bring the needle through at **a** then take a stitch to **b**, bringing the needle back out at **a** without pulling the needle right through. Wrap the thread around the needle, covering the length from **a** to **b**. Pull the needle through and slide the wraps off the needle, easing them down until they are lying on the fabric. Reinsert the needle at **b** to secure the bullion.

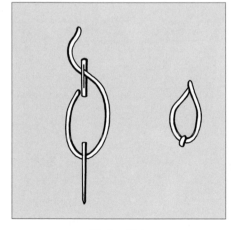

Chain stitch

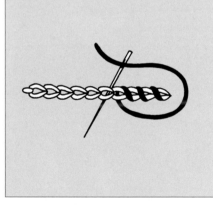

Whipped chain stitch

Detached chain stitch

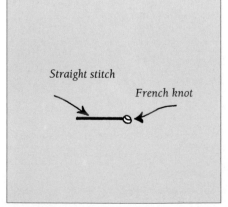

Pistil stitch

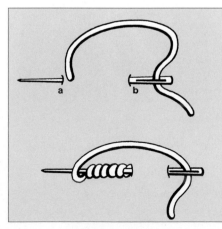

Bullion stitch

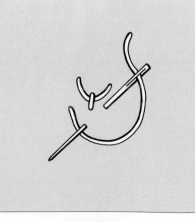

Fly stitch

FLY STITCH

Fly stitch is frequently used for leaves and is worked as an open lazy daisy stitch in ribbon, cotton or wool.

Begin by bringing the needle through from the back or just to the left of where you wish to place the stitch.

Reinsert the needle one stitch length away to the right and take a small stitch back to the centre, keeping the point of the needle over the ribbon, cotton or wool. Pull the needle through and secure the stitch with a small vertical stitch.

FISHBONE STITCH

Work one straight stitch at the end, extending it slightly over the outline. Begin working stitches alternately to the left and right of the centre, overlapping them in the centre as shown.

STEM STITCH

Stem stitch is commonly used for outlines and, as the name implies, is mostly used for working the stems on flowers. Simply take a long stitch, bringing the needle out approximately half a stitch length back. Repeat this procedure along the required length, keeping the ribbon beneath the needle.

FEATHER STITCH

Very much like fly stitch, feather stitch is a pretty way to define a line. Begin at the top of the line and make alternate slanting stitches, pulling the needle through over the working thread.

DETACHED BUTTONHOLE STITCH

Work one row of buttonhole stitch on the edge. Work successive rows, attaching each one to the preceding row only.

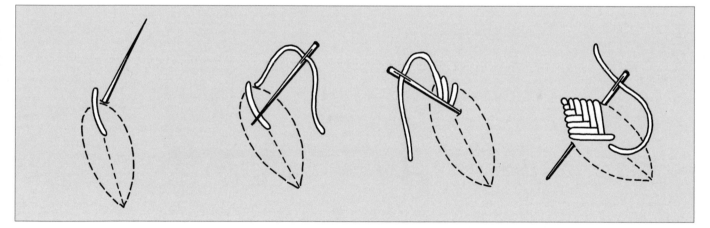

Fishbone stitch

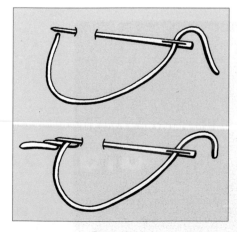

Stem stitch

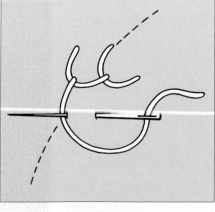

Feather stitch

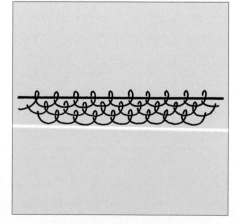

Detached Buttonhole stitch

FRENCH KNOT

Bring the needle up through the fabric where you wish the knot to sit. Wind the thread once around the needle. Gently pulling the thread tight, reinsert the needle at the point of exit and pull the thread through. Bring the needle up through the fabric ready for the next French knot.

BACK STITCH

Bring the needle out at **a** and take a stitch back to **b**, bringing the needle out at **c**. Continue in this manner along the row.

HEMSTITCH

Bring the needle up through the fabric in the hem and take a small stitch as shown (1), bring the needle out a little way along. Work a back stitch (2), then take a small stitch back into the hem (3). Continue in this way along the length of the hem.

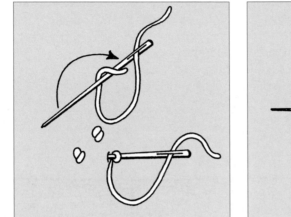

French knot

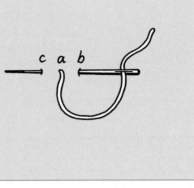

Back stitch

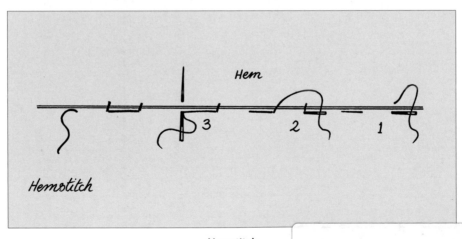

Hemstitch